Martin Willitts Jr.

SELECTED POEMS

FUTURECYCLE PRESS

www.futurecycle.org

Cover photo of stones in a river by Chris F; cover and interior design by Diane Kistner; Gentium Book Basic text and Cronos Pro titling

NOTE

Except for stylistic differences, the poems appear as published in the represented collections.

Library of Congress Control Number: 2024938239

Published by FutureCycle Press
Athens, Georgia, USA

ISBN 978-1-952593-51-2

Contents

from
UNFOLDING OF LOVE

from
HARVEST TIME

from
ALL WARS ARE THE SAME WAR

NEW POEMS

Foreword

I first met my friend, Martin Willitts Jr., through one of his poems.

Turns out it was his first published poem. It appeared in the Happiness Holding Tank in 1974, a publication out of Michigan State University helmed by a beloved professor, writer and hotrod aficionado named Albert Drake.

Turns out I was the selection committee member who plucked it from the slush pile and proclaimed it worthy of publication. After the poem was passed from person to person and eventually into the waiting hands of Mr. Drake, it was unanimous. This Martin Willitts Jr. was a true poet whose work needed to be shared with the world.

In truth, I'd fallen in love at first sight with Martin's work. I copied down his return address and began corresponding with him. And then, within the next year, I rode on a Greyhound bus to meet him where he lived in Syracuse, New York, on my way to the Bread Loaf Writers Conference where I had won a grant.

Martin took me to see the Letchworth Waterfalls and wrote a beautiful poem about the day for me to cherish.

Bread Loaf was amazing and stoked the fires of my love for poetry.

And then.

What most poetry professors warn you about happened to both of us: the unexpected twists and turns of living. At 18, I skedaddled out of Detroit, bound for California. Martin suffered PTSD from his Army stint as a combat medic in the Vietnam War. I lived in a false girl-boy relationship with a closeted gay man in San Francisco for two years. Martin married happily, losing his wife to cancer. I met my soulmate on Valentine's Day in 1982. Martin continued honing his poetry and sharing it with an appreciative audience.

We lost touch with each other.

And then came Facebook. We rediscovered each other there.

Now, 50 years after I held his first published poem in my hands, he has chosen me to write the Foreword to his first book of Selected Poems.

What an honor.

How can I describe his work? It's "accessible" like the work of Billy Collins. It has surprise endings like the work of Mary Oliver. It's full of depth and Nature like the work of Ralph Waldo Emerson.

But Martin's work transcends mere comparison. It weaves together threads of life, love, loss, and longing into a tapestry that speaks directly to the soul.

Each poem is a journey, inviting the reader to explore the depths of human experience and the vastness of the universe.

In his poetry, Martin captures moments of beauty and pain with equal measure, infusing each word with a profound sense of truth. His verses resonate with authenticity, drawing readers into worlds both familiar and unknown. Whether he's reflecting on the natural world, exploring the complexities of human relationships, or delving into the depths of his own psyche, Martin's poetry never fails to leave a lasting impression.

But perhaps what sets Martin's work apart most is its unwavering honesty. He bares his soul on the page, unafraid to confront life's uncertainties and ambiguities head-on. Through his poetry, he reminds us that even in our darkest moments, there is beauty to be found, and that within every heartache lies the seed of hope.

As I reflect on the journey that has led us here, from that chance encounter with a poem to this momentous occasion, I am filled with gratitude. Gratitude for Martin's friendship, for his unwavering dedication to his craft, and for the opportunity to share his remarkable poetry with the world.

So, to you, dear reader, I say: prepare to be moved, to be inspired, and to be forever changed by the words of Martin Willitts Jr. His poetry is a gift, and I am honored to have played a small part in bringing it to you.

—*Patty Mooney*

from
SEARCHING FOR WHAT
IS NOT THERE

National Ecological Award
Hiraeth Press, 2013

Searching For What Is Not There

Looking into a lake, things are elsewhere, off-
center as love when it first enters and leaves.

There is a shimmer of fish,
not where the line drops, but in an angle

frustrating as rejection. Our boat sinks and rises
heaving on the lake's chest. It takes everything in

and gives it back, reflecting on that moment
sighing in insightful serious tones.

*

I find a stone soothed by its passing.
I am reassured life remains constant and moving.

Everything is replaced.
Everything is a message for interpretation.

I dip my hands into the water, break
the sheen of surface into its translucent skin.

*

It is strange, isn't it, how objects find each other?
The alabaster water finds the land.

There is listening among the cattails. A raven
studies intently at its own reflection of dark-blue feathers.

You edge at the water waiting for it to move.
Some feeling in me ripples when you call my name.

*

What we see is not what they seemed at first.
Reflection and new light make differences in what they are.

When you reach into water, what you try to get
lies elsewhere. Who am I to judge what is clear

or not? What we see now is different. When I look again
you are still there, dissipated into rain,

hesitant as a migration searching for something better.
It is the staying that seems strange and right.

*

A journey begins as the sun takes off,
bunches of feathers remaining in a nest of branches.

Fish strike out at small things making ripples
moving towards us. Everything moves closer.

Canoes paddle into shore, in wavering heat.
Gulls circle and lift like hearts.

What was not there before,
is there now.

Rain

> "He grabbed a storm out of a sea and threw it down on the canvas" —Guy de Maupassant about Monet.

Brushstrokes of perpendicular sun-spray
splash yellow on white cove cliffs—rain
is coming. Felt, rather than seen.
Degrees drop—fleeting and introverted—
then there is a hush before things happen.
What part of *this* or *anything* is ever expected?

Strange gray affects rock, cloud-rush,
gathers pitchforks of rain.
There is heaviness of air, blinding light,
before things break. There is an elusive feeling
you know what will happen next.
Premonitions come true.

Nothing penetrates.
Then, rain—echoes on waves.

Nothing is identifiable
in the downpour
from jugs of endless gray waters.
Raindrops splat into broken eggs.

We watch through a streaked window
as below, water runoffs
have nowhere to go. They coalesce.
They vacate everything in the way.
Water sieves through glass.

A storm is withering inside.

Spring

The world is estranged from itself
in this remote area of forbidden cast-off rain-dust
and experimentally rushed-tidal plunge,
wild, primitive land-washes,
the nature of storms is studied.

We are dissatisfied with the lack of explanations.

Rocks are beaten and submerged under painful water.
Blurred white skies are not distinct from distances.
Gray monotonous clouds formulate, then rain in light.
Rain careens through, transmitting atmosphere.
Individual areas have different amounts of rain-drench.
It rains as a Debussy composition.

After rains pass, ceaseless recovery commences.

Too Soon the Clouds of Disenchanted Rains Will Be Upon Us

Too soon the clouds of disenchanted rains will be upon us
filled with reddish-orange Maple leaves
in the harvest moon-lit skies.
In that silence breathes the darkness extending into a languished sigh.
There is nothing about flowers.
There is nothing in the graying wrinkled clouds
of those brown corn stalks of light.
Too soon, the steps will turn ashen white.
If there is anything behind these closed drapes of days,
it is the knowledge things will come and go without me.
The world does not require much from me.
If I was to die tomorrow or the next, there would be no difference.
In the silence afterwards, there are flocks heading away.
In the silence after that, these are the breathless winds.
In the moments of stillness after that, there is the resting hand
upon what it means to be human, to say what is not easy to say,
to consider the long-standing stirring within us.

March

It's rain-making.

Something permanent in the stone steps
is repelling rain. It stops me short.
Makes me draw in my breath,
count my blessings.

It is cold, this steady rain.
But, in your heart, there, it is bristling with love.
You are writing words from March rain.
It is enough to bruise the stone of any heart.
This kind of drenching can fly
into the landscape of your bones.

Gathering Shells

I went early to the sandy beach,
before dark completely rendered itself useless,
when ink-blue meets pink and yellow partitions open.

After last spume of high tide had withdrawn,
its last loud lament, receding, I went to search for shells,
to see if any remained and how many.

There was disappointment. All were broken, alone,
glittering like mica, into so many particles
nothing remained to be identified—

only rare fish smells in cool wet sand.
I had come all this way for nothing.
Where had the souvenir shop found theirs?

I could gather the decimated shells.
There is acceptance in what I had been given.
All this life-and-death is belonging and openness.

Gardening in Georgia Clay

I built a garden on riverbank Georgia red clay: hard dirt
used to make pottery
and not quite right for planting.

In that indeterminate soil was shale ledge, fragments
of tonsil-shaped shells, and coarse beach sand
with particles and filaments from a factory
long reduced to brick, sparkling as night full of fireflies,

I excavated; hands covered with shell-shocked fire ants
biting their discomfort. My hands became swollen
and inflamed for weeks, welded shut,
and almost palsied, stiff as a trowel.

I learned the hard facts then: wear leather gloves
thick as determination.

The information on the seed packets
of how-to-do, what conditions and starting periods
were best and when it was too late, what zone I was in,
where does the frost stop,
when to expect if you follow instructions
carefully, how to determine failure.

After several growing seasons, after several dry seasons
when dirt clumped into afterthoughts,
after several on-going drenching seasons
when soil ran as rivulets taking everything with it
including the seeds, reason, and a watering can,
I soon knew enough of failure.

Failure followed me to work, punching out
my need to re-locate. Failure influenced the temperature
of divorce and the refusal to re-pollinate.
It washed out anything I wanted to hold onto.
It was impossible to manage as the red clay.

Yes, I know a thing or two about failure.
I also know about the joy of seeing the first sprout,
the warm wash of tomato-colored suns,
and sometimes, sometimes, the impulsive clay
was just enough to retain moisture,
just enough for the self-seeding *Forget-Me-Nots*
to remember what they were supposed to do.

And in those moments, I would remove the garden gloves,
head into the house, knowing what I had to do.

Wildly Preaching Among Sunflowers

Van Gogh wanted to be a preacher
to spread the good word, harvesting
both field hands and the merchant,
with all the fever, with all the joy of birds,
converting everything, even the lichen.
But it was not to be.
He could not mold prayer, like a baker into bread.
He felt betrayed by his lack—his faithlessness.
His cold eye turned inward: *I am not worthy.*
He did not like what he saw. A man
whose hands wanted something other than a bible.

He would have flogged himself,
but his weakness was that of a newborn calf.
What good were his words?
Everything was so unattainable.

He thrashed around in the fields,
wrestling with himself—and losing.
When he exhausted himself, he lay in a field of sunbursts.
Sunflowers stared with one eye, like a half-blind god,
praising him for trying. Moments of color
passed into him as sacraments.
He knew then, what he had to do.

He stumbled from one vision to another
for the next ten years, painting what he clearly saw,
even if it was disturbing, transitory, and elating.

His hands had the transformative power of sunflowers.

Seeing Like Never Before

"What have you done with your eyes?"
—Antonio Machado

One day a thin veil lifted from my eyes.
Cherry blossom petals covered the world
in a blanket of pink whispers.
My skin felt a Presence like never before.
A swarm of crawling bees were laying honey
as bricks of dreams.
Poems rise out of well water, in mists.
My eyes were seeing things meant to be seen.
Now I can fall back into myself,
into a new body. One that dances.
One that has more colors than I know what to do with.

The Sounds of Color

"I want a red to be sonorous, to sound like a bell"
—Pierre Augusté Renoir

There is an effect if light on an object
juxtaposes tints as to make colors alive
and quiver, as if the surface was breathing.
I often hear this, although I am losing my hearing.
I hear color altering—it is not always bells.
Sometimes, they warn like crows warring over a carcass.
Sometimes, they jangle like cow bells returning.
Sometimes, they are water snuggling against a canoe.
Sometimes, they haggle over nothing and everything
like at an open bazaar where someone is handling
a silk scarf before wearing on their head.
The sound of color speaks with authoritative words.
They converse with sensuality like a whispering lover
whose words reach inside you, tingling and joyous.
It is not always so tonally red,
although I can read the surface
easily as a capstone or an anecdote of bronze sunsets.
What should you have me make of such intensity?
Such laboring? To gain, what?—heaven?
I am deluged in their songs of praise.
And what should I not be caught up in?—the adoration?
And why should I ignore it, when I can't?
I am a newcomer to these sounds.
Or perhaps, more like a beachcomber
finding what remains when the tides recede.
When I hear what others do not, I am blessed!
And in this, I am closer to what I need to hear.
Sometimes, it is too much for just one person.
Sometimes, it just begins to be enough.
The red winds of music are bells in my heart ringing.

Astronomy Lesson about Love

I would like to say we share the same night star view;
but that is not true. We are more than time zones apart.
Any further away, you would not search for me.

I know you will not read this. You will tear up the envelop
once you see the zip code. Once you know it is from me,
your hatred will return and the distance will extend further.

But isn't this fierce anger from love? Those stars
revolve regardless how you feel. You cannot stop them
any more than you can stop me from trying.

I would like to say you will get over your anger;
but this too is a lie. A black hole is swallowing truth.
When star gazing, you do not find love.

It is when you read letters from former lovers,
you find elliptical orbits. I would like to say many things;
but you would not listen, spinning away.

Futility is the curvature of the horizon,
knowing we cannot see beyond
our own need or suffering.

Love has its own gravitational pull
as well as its own course and sometimes
it is not going in the same direction as we are.

I would like to say a lot of things;
but they are not necessarily true.
So, I say nothing. I write asteroids of letters.

I suspect that if you looked into the night sky
it would be cloudy, no moon, and empty
as mail not opened. You would not hear me.

You are going about your business, perfectly content,
while I am mooning, full of lack of gravity,
on a path that I have no control over.

How happy must be the person
who cares less about astronomy,
and cares more about the gravity of love.

Repairs and More Repairs

a ladder against a house
is a man needing a crutch
about to repair
the roof of the world,
hammering all day if necessary

returning shadows to the garden,
sweeping pebbles until they glow,
going on like normal
if there is any getting back to it

Ile Aux Fleurs

Based on the painting by Monet

There is nothing unusual about standing in wildflowers near a river.
Across the way, blue shadows of trees are thin as smokestacks.
There is nothing that moves anything, but everything is moving.

The river vibrates. The wind hums with katydids.
The clouds meander like geese heading elsewhere in no hurry.
The wildflowers stir, shaken, and flush with stillness.

There is nothing unusual about moving on.
There is nothing special to keep one here, if they are in a hurry.
There is always somewhere to go, something we have to do,

someone is waiting for us, somewhere a job we started
is still undone, a ferry boat is about to cross,
someone will miss it, there are secrets someone will whisper.

We stay. We decide to continue. It is getting late.
We agree and stay longer than we intend.
We stay and wonder why have to go anywhere.

Nature

We are immersed in nature, ceaselessly painting
with anticipation in the orchestra of wildflowers,
for those things hidden under low-lying bushes
bring forth the essence of fact—

that all things encircle us, formed by light,
in the movement of air,
whether it is still or ruffled as a river,
where everything graces our wonderment,
smells buzzing, colors soaked in dew,
transparent senses brush us,

either with winter hoarfrost, or southern heat
stretched out like a stroked cat,
or flashes of sunlight
as dragonflies in the trembling mysterious forest,
or emanating from the keening suburbs,
or from the factories leaning their smokestacks
against the fractured atmosphere—

if we ever live long enough, let us enjoy
these enflamed fluctuations of light
with trickles of indigo and absorbing blues.

The River of Forgetfulness

Note: It is one of the five rivers of the Greek underworld.

There are memories we wish we can forget,
we put so deeply into ourselves
we forget that they are there. Memory becomes a river
without a bridge. It remembers dark things.
The current of the mind is too swift
to swim across. We can only wish
for life to be different. But the results are not.

After a war, some of us return
but we never make it back.
Some of us return wounded,
a body part missing,
we see things
we never want to talk about.
This river leads to nowhere.

We do not want to bath in that water,
drink endlessly, carry it in canteens.
Instead, we are on a ferry boat,
as the shore keeps pulling further away.

Touch Is Something We All Need

"I love pictures which make me want to stroll in them,
if they are landscapes, or caress them, if they are nudes"
—Pierre Augusté Renoir

Better yet, I want to caress a landscape.
I want the impact of the translation of light
upon the waves ingrained on a tree bark.
I want to trace my fingers on those deep furrows
to hear what they have seen all those watchful years.
I will massage and break the tension
like a rise of startled quail, or the break of air at sunrise.
In the tree's branches, trying to hold things still
long enough for us to enjoy seeing them:
a song of a pinfeather, a knit of string and sprigs,
an egg holds its secrets in blue-speckled breathes.

Below, flowers curl as earlobes,
hearing us to approach,
waiting for us to inspect them for perfection,
a craftsman with absolute standards.
I want to stroke across the flower's chambers,
like soft-carpeted footsteps
approaching a lover, as if I want to touch
the light in their hair before it fades
to find the undertones.

In the naked light,
everywhere contains field sprays,
like dappled skin in transferred light,
like it has been waiting all morning
for us to kiss them with the lightest kiss possible,
not waking up or startling anything,
and still be a kiss. Light waits for us to find it—
in this exposed moment, that is
if we are not too embarrassed to look.

Look!
—it is blushing as a rose petal in the arousal of light.
How it purrs and stretches, satisfied,
as it slides into awakening.

Trace Evidence

1.

There is a moment, in darkness,
when dark changes, as it hesitates
trying to resist daybreak, shimmers,
purple as a bruise, losing the fight.

This last black upon shaded-black
is when clouds start to become noticeable.
The horizon is differentiated

What was hidden is emerging.
We can begin to see where land begins and sky ends.
Light is still taking its time getting here.
But it is coming—at its own cumbersome pace.

All things must change—
like a battered rush of crackles changing directions.

Those impulsive birds make a clap
as they rise
pulling pink snails of light into the sky.
Leaves darken with green light,
no longer blending with hills.

We wake to the alarm clock of cicadas.

There is a fundamental sameness and differences,
Yellow-redness is the last thing of morning,
as drawstrings lifting dark.

2.

When the sun ascends the ladder of hills,
is it replaced in the absence of evidence?

Where are you in this darkness?
This beginning light?
What trace evidence of yourself is left behind?
If you say you did the same thing today as yesterday,
you would be wrong.

No matter how mundane we are, or think we are,
we never have the same experience every day.
For every single day, things are happening,

Send out evidence you care.
Send out evidence, that in the end, that we are evidence.
Ascend the rugged ladder of hills as a morning song,
using a lantern of moon.

Lasting

A final dark-spotted leaf
is folding its mystery in purple, still attached
to branch trying to shake it loose
into the crunching fallen colors, brittle in air.

It did not want to let go, dying
and resurrecting in its next stage.
Dirt was under some leaves, loving in the fall.
The leaf clung to what it knew.

It did not want to go into the unknown.
Soon it would have no choice. It would be gone.
I, too, would be gone. My staying is not possible.
My returning to the soil is welcomed and waiting.

My heart is straight with the universe.
For some, it is the end. For me—what a beginning!
In the excellence of seasons and weather,
we cannot change inevitability. We can only embrace it.

During A Long Journey

The road becomes hypnotic,
speaking of moments that are passing;
like sirens, about collection pass due,
how leaves are collected into soil,
the way clouds take away and give.

You are tight as hands on a steering wheel.

You pull over to rest.
You let the world rush by you,
a flight of restless birds.

You lower the side window.
A breeze from somewhere distant, visits.
It has been waiting just for you.
The breeze always has been waiting for you.

It takes a while to relax
into the heartbeat around you.
Some moments should never be hurried,
like a seed that takes time
in silent prayer before awakening.

You are under a tree.
You start to wonder what kind of tree it is.
But the name relaxes within you.
You let go,
then you let go again,
and then the day turns its page on you.

Singing in the Apron of Stars

I did it. I sang full-throttle
while the neighbors glared suspiciously,
and it felt *right,* annoyingly *right,*

the word *"proper"* did not fit into the scales,
nor *"consideration"* for melody or harmony,
or if the words were well chosen,
or if anyone listened to me,

I was liberated, for even a moment,
to do what my heart knew instinctually *right,*
and I was doing what I should be doing.

I was clipping the hedges with hymns.

Caterwauling, one neighbor judged,
but I could not help it,
I could not bear my silence anymore,
I needed to join the choir of nightingales
singing well past bedtime
into the apron of stars

I could not help it; my longing was so great,
so impetuous, I could not stop the ocean of song,
nothing could stop me, not dusk,
not coal-dust night

my throat came down with laryngitis,
until I croaked from my swollen belly

I sang, even in my sleep,
on bed sheets of music
beyond and into the *A cappella* of new mornings.

from
HOW TO BE SILENT

FutureCycle Press, 2016

How to Be Silent

Into the evening and beyond, swooping
nightjars chase moths. The sound of them,
less than silence, is hush-spiraling.
If this be the color of tree bark,
then what are those long-tipped wings
sliding across the moorlands out of the brackens—
with no more noise than a prayer kept to ourselves?
Nightjars conceal themselves from daylight,
and now they are after the large flying insects,
like there is no tomorrow. And they should know,
belonging more to darkness than to the known,
moving with suddenness. Into the evening
and beyond, where light is already disappearing,
are whispers of sounds that are less than whispers.
We want to reduce the universe into simple concepts,
into a bird touching silence. We want distilled silence—
to reach into that speechless sense of wonder.
We want to suppress fears that worry at our bones.
Those darting nightjars, a smothering darkness,
stopping sounds into insignificance, shush the stars.
The nightjars make the quiet possible with their presence.
They put an end to panic moving through the night.
Nightjars encourage silence into happening.

Being in the Presence

Being in the Presence is more than the here and now.
It is falling into the totality of silence;
hearing that secret personal message;
reaching from the mind to toes, a current of Love;
shaking loose darkness
into pure Light;
feeling lighter—a shuffling of belief.
It is then, and only then, we're transformed
into a cloud of welcoming birds.

What Happens When in Stillness

There is a long walk from here to the pasture
where events are happening without you.
On the way, notice what you never did before.
Wait for the moment of no sound. You will hear this,
the under-breath of reverberation.
Stillness will stir the winds into heartbeats.
Wait patiently as a mountain shoving against clouds.
Wait until movement stops, which is impossible.
Wait for when the impractical becomes expected.
Remain in this emptiness. This is when you are in
the presence of anticipation. This is being within
unspoken prayer. This is what it is like to be flame.

What It Is Like to Go into Silent Meditation

There were crabs and small fish in a hollow tidal pool.
Their life was fleeting temporary memories
into the left-behind, struggling into quietness.

How many of us feel this ultimate frustration—
that we are abandoned. But sometimes, winds return
from a place I can barely imagine.

How uncontrolled life is. How arbitrary it is:
moon-pull or merciless jury; stone heart or mercy. Which?
In the quest of meditation, the heart rests at a dangerous level.

There is a risk of not returning when we go this deep—
into a silence of our own choosing. There is the unnatural
amazement of letting loose and returning to an unchanged world.

This Pond Has Clear Imaginings

The pond wants to empty itself
of all earthly concern, to reach
a unique, passing insight,

a clarity, unspoiled by carp or
freckled tadpole, splaying across
the water in long, lingering, laziness.

It wants more of itself, more purity
of the divine, the inspired,
to be thoughtful and thought-provoking,

to *twingle* when disturbed, to blush
when reflecting upon a sunrise,
to stand perfect as a heron becoming light.

It wants seven impossible changes
before waking; it yawns serenely,
holding its own breathlessness.

Psalm

Whenever I never know what to say to you,
compassion becomes a torrent of mountain rain.
The silence afterwards is incomprehensible.

In the room of stillness,
the separation between darkness and light
is writing a message on my heart.

I trace the etching with a finger.
Its grove is gouged from pressing so hard,
impressing its importance as on a stone tablet.

A strange echo of loons' crosses water-light.
It is the abandonment of rushes in marsh grass,
the disturbances felt in wing-spread.

These disturbances go on even when no one sees them.
I would translate what they mean to the milkweed—
but silence is always here.

White birches rift in sinew winds. All twist
in fifths through twenty minutes of improvisation,
searching for the right grace note, that perfect pitch.

Peace is not found in the swells, or rowboats of clouds,
nor in the nave of a church where the choir practices.
All permanence is shaken as the sensitive bush shrivels.

All belief is taken. We do not seem to care.
The music is gone as white wings of breath.
We never understand the dark underside of clouds.

Listen

There are days when we should be outside,
in the map of fields, trying to locate the whelks,
the poppy sunrise, the ocean
of wild yellow roses, or the rabbit days
hurdling over the rise to where we have not been.
The world is rekindling its spirit.
It's happening without you.
You sit in the uncomfortable room
while the natural world is restoring its commitment.
Messages scuttle as hermit crabs. Birch trees
are mentioned in passing.

We cannot always enter yesterday like it is a cabin.
It is boarded up. The latch was never repaired.
The wire mesh screen door speaks softly about you.
It is in the pine scent of emptiness,
in the cupboards where not one memory is stored
except stillness.

What are you doing here when you can be out there?
You can fall halfway between dreams and never be
where you need to be. You need to find the deer-run.

If there is a wind, it is the same wind in the shape of weeds,
hunching over wildflowers. It enters you
as a flare of poetry, connecting ideas
you never imagined. Light strikes your face,
making it into a settling moon. Now listen.

Psalm

All day, inside me, your voice was saying,
wake up. But I was not sleeping.

Wake up, you insisted. But I continued
to nibble at life.

At night, your voice would not let me sleep.
Someday, I will rest, but not today.

I am stirring. Your voice is gnawing inside me.
I have been rowing in circles and did not know it.

Tor House

Robinson Jeffers was sunning on granite,
lying skyward, composing on paper
the idea of rocks hewn into uneven squares,
because the world is not perfect. These rocks
would be the meditation of silence. They would
make an Irish castle with a turn-gate, as a pathway
to walls of poems filled with hawk-joy, loam kisses,
lichen freckles, dizzy with word-blend.

The rocks would remember heron shadows,
concrete and isolated, in tune with nature
and heart. He would ask the rocks
for permission. He would carry them over the barrens,
beyond the periphery where surf collided with shore.

Over the promontory, he'd pass the outcrop of sea-grass,
where the bitter place of winds coil and spring,
away from where water does not think
before it smashes. This house would become lyric
of love, where to touch stone reminded him of love.

He would build low to the ground, to take the worst
of storm and loss. He would sing like terns in swoop
and sway, wheeling cursives of love in breakwater sky.
Granite walls would be in perfect pitch. He'd read aloud
into star-spray, use block and tackle lift. Not easy,
this work; not prideful either, the work of hands.
Where else could love feel the earth quake of heart?

Mending the Net

Based on the painting by Thomas Eakins, 1881

We gather as a community, prepared to mend.
Forgiveness is in the air.
If we do not restore trust, it will haunt us as a storm moving in.
The fabric of love demands patching.
We begin our solemn task, bent to this renovation.

We gather at *The Meeting Tree*—a place where we head
after a storm to make sure all is accounted for.
Anyone missing is a tangling of the net.
Let no one be lost. Anyone misplaced shall be found—
let not one body be mislaid.

We will spread our net far and wide.
We congregate at this wisp of a tree where our answers
are prayers. We inspect what we have made
and find it maddeningly wanting. There are gaps, rends,
some small as a gull's eye, some are bigger than grief.
The world cannot be repaired without hard work.
Listening to suggestions is fishing of a religion.
Without a community, there is no sharing.

If we lack that, we swim as minnows within the silence.
We are making what was broken into whole.
Fishing has taught us patience.
We throw away what we do not need.

When someone is missing, we diminish into the accumulating loss.
We pursue a horizon as it stays far ahead,
uncertain as to when to haul in our cast nets.
We rely on instinct to stop and repair what is needed.

It is like knowing when to pray
and when it will not suffice. We are entangled
in the sharing, as words swim by too small for catching.
We are never done with mending promises in the sky-net.

Psalm

As close as any two molecules
of skin, I am to you.

During any uncertainty
of this truth, even when
you are not here,
you remind me—
love is that unusual.

Love is any number of birds
hiding in a winter bush
anyone can see,

when they take off,
it is like when you leave—
always that quickness.

As far away as you are now,
you are near.

Any impossibility,
you are.

Psalm

How wonderful the Spirit—
the promise of the gladiolas
yellow in the enlightened air
smelling new mysteries.

What I need is in the garden:
Kneeling into the deepness of the ground
speaking to me through my palms
so my hands can see what the earth tells me.

All I need waits here, within reach:
the watering can full of delicious tears:
the purple pansies with their secrets:
the tiny wild strawberries taking over a stump.

I gather these into rain that is not raining. A song
of solace. A dance of fireflies like meteor showers.

I bring them to my nose, like bit garlic. Inhale,
breathing like a desperate man. Like a woman
who cannot get enough of the light.

So, here it is. I am sharing it with you.
It is the moon leaving its promises.
It is the shifting of the unknown.
It can have wings if it wants.

In the Presence of Absence

In the Presence of Absence, we find
our own lacking or our erasure.
Most people would hover around this loss,
a bottomless chasm,
but I leap in.

I can tell you this:
it does not go straight through earth
into the Endlessness.

There is no hard or soft landing. And for all I know,
I am still free-falling.

I feel hands under me, lowering me, gently,
all the while being told: *Trust.*
So, I do.

I am no longer falling or rising; I am neither here,
or there, or anywhere.

I am in the Belonging, in the Longing;
I am accepted for who I am:
imperfect, curious, searching, believing.

The Incessant Knocking

Listen. The Lover is knocking,
but not on a door—in our hearts.
If we answer, what will we find?
If we sleep through the incessant knocking,
what will we miss?

When I first heard this tapping,
I opened the windows and shouted,
waking the robins, the dogs,
the moon, the crickets. Lights went on.
Everything was disturbed.

My secret Lover wished to be a secret,
so my Lover went away like a tidal wave,
like a dream.

The next time the Lover came visiting,
I was more prepared.
It was like finding Light in a dark closet.

Rapture

An assemblage of birds is hiding in its own calling.
Its music hides in the raspberries.
Thick sheet music of fog hovers low to a changing ground,
while above is autumnal-harsh light.
The light's astonished response is to migrate.

It's unexpected, yet anticipated,
thumbing throughout the departure of days. This calling
becomes interwoven, damp and memorized differently,
back to the way life used to be.

This unsung chattering continues
into redness of a cold morning.
We hear emptiness afterwards,
piercing as the deep hill.
In the low-sung air, a burn-off, unravels.

Then, what calls?
No umber sky being called forth.
Who speaks in silence? The ground flutters and flits.

Music, a waiting river, moves out of intense hunger.
Scarlet birds blend into bleeding, burnished skies.
Their shadows imagine songs impossible to sing. Once over,
the singing does not end: a river roving on.

I believe this amber forest was always this red,
its leaves flapping. A clap of thunderheads
is a clump of teeming cardinals, slapping out of branches
up into the aggregation, dredging up brightness,
bristling with dew, releasing themselves from guilt into sunrise,
disintegrating into an epiphany, scattered as weather.

This is no normal awakening from silence into song.
A hush from the hickories was astonished in the afterlight.
It is in the blaze of foglift.

The Universe Has a Sermon about Remembrance

If I could not hear,
the marshes would send their breezes
full of loons and drakes.
If I could not speak, silence would speak for me:
becoming yellow roses, incandescent star-falls,
grammar of memory,
adjectives of landscapes.

The world would not abandon me.
Love would be compound sentences
in traces of uncommon space.
I would know more than I do now.
I would know parables of Love.

In this, there is no vacuum of oblivion.
There is only promise.

We Should Be Disturbed

We should be disturbed—
wanting to climb into cherry blossoms when it snows pink—

proclaiming love loudly in the throes of love,
a plaintive call from clouds.

The world should be full of noise,
shaking sleeves of night-shivers,

making a calligraphy of love,
a thrush sharing its four-notes to no one in particular.

In this constant creating,
the hibiscus moon hides behind a flock of star-swans.

Psalm

There is a passing, calling me from somewhere.
My blood feels it—
starting over the wheat fields—like a hand.
This is an immediate transitory passage
from this world into the next world.
This is a loss in which we cannot imagine.
At our quieter moments we will hear this calling
and respond.

Will we be receptive to this calling?
Or will we continue to close our ears?
And if we look, what will we see?
Will we see what we are meant to notice?

It is impossible to ignore this calling.
We are in the forever.
Accept the emptiness of our hearts,
sing back to this calling. Enter into it,
feeling the weight of our own losses;

then, we are graced. Now turn
to enjoy the richness of living, fully.
Life is a long preparation of saying goodbye.
This inevitable leaving is what we all must do.

Psalm

"How shall the heart be reconciled/ to its feast of losses?"
—Stanley Kunitz, *The Layers*

I have seen people die,
watching them turn into light,
catching it as they go
to a place so full of Light
it can always take more.

I, too, want to hold light.

I have moved through continents of lives,
numb to the world around me,
forgetful of what is important.

Please remind me
if I ever forget again,
if I forget to appreciate what I have.

We slip in and out of life
like we were trying on shoes
to see which will fit us.

I, too, want to hold onto light
like it was air.

Whose cheek did I first touch?
What first unknown door did I open?

What did I leave behind?

If I leave one message behind,
let it be love.
Let it be an everlasting love
like tender rain in you.
Let it give you light to hold in your hands.
Let it be love.

Early Autumn at Itako

Based on a woodblock by Kawase Hasui
Note: Itako are blind shaman

Our boat of ghostly rains merges deliberately
into a stream of darkness. It is a song
of settling-down, the kind a mother coos to her baby.

The river messages, and its skin ripples.
The moonlight adds a part of this song.
Noise whispers across water as a dwindling star.

Let go of the oars. Let them slip into the evening,
and trust that you will be taken somewhere.
Lack of trust ripples that fade.

The oar is already into the lost. We are barely moving,
and yet we are moving, like a mother swaddling a child
into a blanket of clustered stars.

What is the difference, when we are so loved,
that the wrapping takes the length of a song and not less?
The melody crosses a lake with the same current as moonlight.

When we grow older, our songs unravel their wrappings,
the boat lists, the stars are further from our cupped hands,
but our whisper is a mosquito heard in the absence of a lake.

What startling secret can we let drive in stilled water?
When a distant voice calls us to come home,
will we answer that plaintive cry?

When Stillness Is Heard

There was no one there when I heard a voice.
Haven't you had a strangeness like this?
I did not respond right away, ignoring it,
and its restlessness increased.
I chucked it off as imagination.
Haven't you ignored queasy feelings?
Perhaps the voice was from the empty fields.
But there was stillness in the grass and air.
This uneasiness followed me into the car
and went with me.
The stillness was so quiet.
There was silence in my house.
No sound in the sky. Emptiness in the isolated miles.
The voice persisted.
Ever ignore a message that refused to be ignored?
It was telling me to *enjoy* and *love*.
That message was everywhere it needed to be.
All I had to do was *listen*—then, it was everywhere.

from
DYLAN THOMAS AND THE WRITING SHED

FutureCycle Press, 2017

Daffodils

Daffodil (*Narcissus pseudonarcissus*)

A daffodil bud is seen among the snow,
offering forgiveness. Winter was harsh,
and the brutality of summer is not far away.
We need forgiveness. Surely, after tribulations
there is relief. Already we are gardening dreams.
It had been huddling like an old gray woman
grabbing her shawl, in an underground house,
stirring a promise to return.
Soon its six petals harmonic sense will bring love.

All day, it radiates. Although it has not grown,
you can feel the end of winter, like curtains rustling.
It appeared in the Garden of Gethsemane as relief,
and felt what would happen next. It was also there
for the Roman soldiers who bit its bulb to ease
their wounds, knowing what would happen next.

Now it's here for us, and we do not know what will happen.
We only see so far, and things go pass faster. Tolerance
is easier as we become older, and suffering becomes normal
as our bodies find new ailments. In our dreams we plant.
We are yellow petals caught in a frayed shawl.

In a world uncertain what will happen next,
there are some things we can expect and some we can't.
The snow understands it cannot stand in the daffodil's way.

Dylan Thomas in the Writing Shed in Candle Light

Here in the shed he would write
with light from white fingers
of tapered wax-sloughed votive candles
from a Catholic prayer altar,
while the constellation Altar was fire in the sky.

There were pictures cut from newspapers,
with Greta Garbo in direct center,
who, he argued, had no peer.
There was a picture of collapsed castle ruins
like failed poems, torn after two hundred revisions,
scattering as pigeons in a park.

Here he could look out a window, pull the curtains
as intermission for a play, and see what he was missing.
He would wish to join outside, but he had poems to write
and cigarettes to remove from a used cigar box.
He smoked, dragging every last breath of it.
He might open one of the candy wrappers of sourness
to have the taste of reality on his tongue.

He could look out the window
beyond the shadow of blurring lost to sight.

Entering Dylan Thomas' Writing Shed

Today, I step into his shed,
feel the walls like the inside of a whale,
see the images he left behind
like an archeologist's dream.
I see his tweed suit jacket,
and his chair wears it
like a king might wear a royal robe,
although his jacket moves as a dream
someone else ought to have.

His shed is writing inside me
with tidal waves of words
crunching as small shells under my feet.

I feel Dylan entering me, his hair wavy as terns
in the skull-opened skies. He climbs
my backbone like Jacob's Ladder
or a staircase of a lighthouse
to shine into the worse kind of fog.

Here is a list of vocabulary words,
searching for the precise meaning,
the perfect word, the kind of word
that disappears into a lawyer's contract
everyone signs but no one ever understands.

Here is the moon, the burning end of a cigarette,
the haphazard sketching of seas
changing the handwriting on the sand.
Here I see myself in the reflection of large eyes
staring back, asking where I have been
all these years. I speak as if into a microphone
during a report about a blitzkrieg.
I put on the tweed because it is suddenly cold.

I start to write a couple of words for a poem,
scratch off one word, rumbling the sheet like a shirt
drenched in sweat and lamp smoke.
I stroke my uneven, day-old, unshaven jawbone.

Somewhere, Caitlin is calling. Somewhere,
beaches are calm. Somewhere, fishing boats
head towards home, nets wiggling with stories.

Somewhere, a man thinks he knows me;
he could not be further from the truth.

For while people see me face the salt wind through a window,
no one knows the way to this home.

5 Cwmdonkin Drive, Swansea, Wales

Dylan Thomas' Birthplace

I could look out my bedroom window
to the edge of love.
The bay's curves are a tern in flight
to where I could not go.

I could dream through the day, and dreaming was free.
No boy should give up the comforts of his room
for the unknown,
unless it's a great adventure.

I would lie on my bed and look at the ceiling
like it was a blank sheet of paper
and compose the world around me,
editing carefully, choosing the right words
for the right occasions.
And there were many occasions to come.

I could not know it then, or sense it then
coming for me with opportunists
and tragedies, and the future I could not imagine.

But I was young and foolish like a polished apple.
I had a work of dreaming, and I plowed those fields.

Here my family moved upwards through society,
voices filling the rafters
with vowels. Mine was the timbre of a deep voice,
stilled within me, a secret storm.

I was young and easy then. Not more than a verse.
What could I know of dreaming,
having never exhausted mine? Darkness
was all around the house, coming up the walk,
ringing the doorbell—do not answer it, Mother,
it's me as an adult trying to find my way home.

Dylan Thomas' Chair, Looking Out the Writing Shed

White banners of egrets; lapwings'
slow irregular wingbeats, like a person
having a change of heart;
herons mating for life;
oystercatchers wading on the shore edges,
poking in the sand with long orange beaks;
seals sun tanning on gray rocks,
merging with local color.

The oystercatchers knew this secret:
the world was a bipedal cockle.
If you pried it open
from its hinges
beyond its saltwater taste,
you might find sheen inside
like the inside of a pocket watch
with all the time in the world
to create.

Getting It Right

"To write anything just to let the words and ideas,
the half-forgotten images, tumble on the sheets of paper"
—Dylan Thomas

A villanelle

Do not lose your way for the lack of words.
We are ships losing our way.
We are fragile as paper and hearts stirred.

Loneliness is a thirsty bird.
We need to see what will happen, what life will say.
Do not lose your way for the lack of words.

Your ideas are tumbling like loose boards.
We are stillness across a long bay,
we are fragile as paper and hearts stirred.

Day breaks many backs, greening the dark yards.
Take this hand, these words of blue jays.
Do not lose your way for the lack of words.

We do not need to measure our words in thirds,
where each step is dangerous prey.
We are fragile as paper and hearts stirred.

And what is it, exactly, we think we heard?
Do not lose one moment, one day,
do not lose your way for the lack of words.
We are fragile as paper and hearts stirred.

Echoes of Fern Hill

Based on stained glass by L. Marouf

I am thrilled by light. It reverberates
like a glass of water,
a long, lingering *ting*.

The hills are like this—shimmering shook
ricocheting sound
rigorous as a swim in ice water.

Sound amasses with memories,
heaping upon each recollection,
a concert finding the pinnacle.

And when the audience of trees and hills
folds its program notes,
the silence becomes a different composition.

Though Lovers Be Lost, Love Shall Not

Based on stained glass by S. Healy
A Shakespearian sonnet

We may lose our way from time to time, but not our love.
We may seek what we cannot find, but love finds us.
If we think love has forgotten or abandoned us, shoved
us to the side, it has not. Love is where the winds rush
to find the edge of the earth and find a willing heart.
We shall not forget when we find love or lose love,
nor shall we forget when we find ourselves apart
from love. As new lovers cannot get enough hugs
and seeing clouds in each other's eyes, it never is enough.
We shall lose each other many times; many times, be found.
Keeping love alive seems hard, and it can be rough
to keep the romance. But love is never a line, it is round
cycling moons and suns, rising and falling and kissing.
It never goes away, it is never dormant, never failing.

from
THREE AGES OF WOMEN

Deerbrook Editions, 2017

Sudden Chill

Based on the painting, "Gloucester Farm," by Winslow Homer, 1874

She gave him a ladle of fire-cold spring-water.
He drank loudly and forgot to thank her.
Afterward, water tasted like love ignored.

The hoeing was hot, sweaty work. So, he drank
until his head was numb. He did not notice
the icy-intense stare of a woman ignored too often.

She did not understand his silence.
When a farmer stops working, nothing gets done.
He did not have time. The cows were lowing.

For her, love would be noisy butterflies,
or the moon, half-awake, in the rafters.
It was the fence knocked down by hunters.

It was a paper cutout opening into two hearts.
It meant what it meant.
If she could explain it, it would ruin the meaning.

For him, tomorrow meant more of the same.
He would get up before the rooster. Go out;
milk the cows dry as wheat. Thrash the corn.

Work until his body was a split-rail fence.
Days were numbing. The same everyday-ness.
He would miss how quickly she would flow,

moods like cloud-cover,
her eyes blinking, wide-eyed, and hoping.
He was not cut out for anything else except haying.

She was a frantic heartbeat,
and he was a slow, assured, measured one.
Things mean what they mean. One day, she was gone.

Chances move quickly
and are gone, just as fast. Like a papercut.
Sometimes they just move at their own pace.

Mending More Than Socks

Based on Archibald J. Motley's painting, 1924

She has mended a generation of socks.
She is as old as the waxed fruit in the bowl.
Her hands are furrowed as years in the fields.
There were times when she felt
that she would never be done,
she would find herself repairing the hole in the dark.
She would work in her dreams, always
picking threads of cotton.
I would hear a soft snore, finding her in her chair,
the socks on her lap like sad tired children.
I would try not to disturb her, pulling a blanket up.
She would look at me with woolen eyes,
"What do think you are doing? I am not done."

When she was in a casket like a knitting basket,
I expected her to scold me for coming home late,
for forgetting my skin was nightshades,
for gambling and consulting with shameful women,
for wearing toes through my socks
since I never seem to care how to get new ones.
When I saw her in the coffin with a darning needle in her hand,
I burst into a carnal cry for the years spent wasted.
One of her grandchildren tugged me on the cuff,
"Are you the one she loved as much as sewing?"
I knew then a generation is held together by threads.

Maple and Cedar; Lake George

Based on the painting by Georgia O'Keefe, 1920

*

the end of summer turns phoenix red,
the end of what we left behind, the arrival
of the next—

if we knew then
what we know now

the flames of Alzheimer's would make more sense

instead of letting things go
instead of forgetting ourselves
lost in our own forest—

sometimes, she exhilarated,
it is so perfect
I want to tear it all to pieces

*

she tears out maple roots
before they can settle in,
shakes the ingrown plants,

dirt clings to them like relatives

*

her lover returns
slamming the wire mesh screen cabin door
howling for something to eat

she wants to serve him burnt sienna,
red maple leaves drenched with regret,
the smell of cedar chests

she tears leaves to pieces,
into perfect lies they tell each other

what holds us together? she wonders,
not these loose roots.

*

relatives visit
bringing pass-around meals

closing arguments
about how she was not the perfect host,
not an immaculate housekeeper,
not the right one for him

they were noisy mosquitoes

their voices were leaves
crunching under her sneakers

she was not good enough,
never would be, could not be,
and according to them, not equal in art

perhaps
taking advantage of his fame

she wanted to canoe away from them

Lake George simply was not big enough for them,
the maple trees were not red enough,
the cedars needed more vibrant colors

O'Keeffe paddled all the way to the desert to get away
wondering if it was far enough,
from their impossible high standards.

Pelvis IV

Based on the painting by Georgia O'Keefe, 1944

in violent times
when wars fight over continents
because someone was not content
blue can be such a calm color

when the world reduces to bone
I refuse to stay quiet
on the sidelines
someone must speak out

blue has been here since the beginning
it will still be here
after men are finished with destruction
blue bonnets or bluebells still remain

the spirit resides in blue auras
indigo mountains in haze
cobalt shadows in skulls
when I lift one to the azure sky

all I can see
blue tea kettle steam
poured into a blue cup
slices of blueberry jam in blue light

empty spaces are talking to me
telling me someday wars will end
men will stop their nonsense
be sensible as blue coyote fur

those days seem far away
yet in relative time
close as turquoise rivers or
blue beetles crossing dark navy shadows

The Lawrence Tree

Based on the Georgia O'Keefe painting, 1929
At D.H. Lawrence's house in New Mexico

I would lie for hours on a wooden bench
under a tree, looking up into sky
until it blinked first.

Leaves were spiritual poems
telling of deep longings
on how the world came to be—

how this wooden bench was made,
each swirl, knothole, every smoothed edge—
life is measured precisely.

The tree tells me the sky was made for me,
ingrained inside me
like water inside clouds.

Tonight, there are so many stars,
distance and closeness do not matter,
perspective falls apart miles from here.

If I reach up, I can pull down everything—
loneliness; poems; spiritual stars;
leaves; bird wings; beautiful space.

The Justified Anger

Based on the painting, "Self-Portrait with Monkey,"
by Frida Kahlo, 1938

I stare at you with suspicion
in a jungle of ferns big as sombreros.

There is a baby chimp peering, on my shoulder,
curious, wondering what I hear.

I hear a drunken man rattling a locked door,
or factories on strike against low wages.

I wear a collar of bone to remind me
we all die in a forest, alone, not trusting.

The key does not fit into the keyhole,
it moves my body away from his touch.

When he arrives like this, roaring with tequila,
his black paws peel at my breasts like they were bananas.

When he gets this drunk, he vomits the moon.
I do not trust his excuses.

Soon his hand will smack my face with thunder
and he will be dangerous as a pistol.

Tonight, I will slit his lying tongue,
I will merge into the ferns, alone.

Braids

Based on the painting by Andrew Wyeth,1979

How long do they take to make them?
Hand over delicate hand, twisting them into shape.
It must take all day or more, such raveling.

I am envious of your husband if he is the one that undoes them.
He must take his time unwrapping them
like they were Christmas presents.

He must enjoy untangling your hair as it speaks to him.
The air must be holding its breath.
If only I could have the pleasure

to untie them as knots on a nightgown
slipping slowly down your body,
exposing you and light, light and you.

If there is a God, then he must have created braids,
and rested several days admiring their luster,
their primitive sexuality, and gasped—it's good.

Farm Road

Based on the painting by Andrew Wyeth, 1979

She has turned her back to me
heading back to the fields,
a fairy
who has spent too much time
in the human world
and is about to lose her wings.

She heads to her weather-beaten house
to her bone China
chipped as her chin.

She goes back to her husband
who cannot possibly understand her.

She accepts her fate
as part and parcel of her faith,
written on her hard-scrabble face.

She will set the dinnerware
like she has a thousand times
the same precise way.
Her husband will barely notice.

She will peel potatoes
humming a mindless tune
from memory, toss one
into a boiling pot
asking, does he love me,
does he not.

She will go to bed afterwards,
fold her hands over the down quilt
as he turns off an oil lamp,
the light fading like love.

from
THE UNCERTAIN LOVER

Dos Madres Press, 2018

Alternative Endings

The sky coming for us, and it is not pleased.
The old gossip of rain falls apart into splintered glass.

In each death, there includes an alternative ending.
One of them crinkles into paper birds singing.

In the warehouse of darkness, there are questions.
You can unpack them, but assembled, they are meaningless.

Your breath waits across the street under a streetlight.
It wants to know the value of waiting.

Who knows what small truths hide in a closet afraid?
In another death, a chorus of peepers are trilling in marsh light.

We could be planets of gnats circling a grazing cow.
We could be among the trail of blue flashes.

When designing angels, God thought wistfully of birds
and secondly of men attempting to become birds.

The Uncertain Lover

"I love you as certain dark things are to be loved"
—Pablo Neruda

Who among you understands the guitar? If you do not know
how it makes a woman sway, then you know nothing.

I sing under her balcony as a cricket in a torrid season.
Let others suffer their internal struggles. Not me.

A man can do only so many things badly. Love is one.
I will strum on her neckline until she dances feverishly.

For what is a man, but a musician of the soundless air.
Too many men carry their dares on their lips. Not me.

I had the scent of mistakes from love and not loving well.
I have washed myself until I was no longer alone,

for I find a lack of comfort twisting empty sheets,
uncomfortable as random cards. I want none of this.

Men find gloom is dependable when other things are not.
I am not such a man. I want the light from a certain woman.

Mother to Daughter Talk about Spices

A little bit of this, a dash of that,
no more than a thin dust on your palm.
Spices are precise and imprecise,
just like first love, where a little bit of a kiss
can be delicious as cinnamon. Too much love
can cause heart damage like too much salt.

Too much of a good thing can be simply too much.
Ration love like spices: keep them in hand
but out of reach. A dash of intrigue—
like not showing so much skin—
will inflame his heart, so apply only a dash.
Keep the relationship spicy;
just enough to keep him coming back for more.

A good cook knows how to stir her pot—
what to put in, what to leave out.
A terrible cook will set everything in fire
and have nothing left to show for it.

A woman brings seasoning to her table
and her bed. A man brings an appetite.

Promise Me

> "When I die, I want your hands on my eyes"
> —Pablo Neruda

When I die, cover me with briar roses
so that I am reminded how painful life can be
without you in my arms. In my green heart
strides the ache of a man carrying heavy, wooden milk pails.

When I die, wrap me in linen from your tears—
the kind of rapids that wash away worry,
the kind that drips dew from rose petals,
the kind of tears that rosters hear when they are lonely.

When I die, marry quickly and fiercely like we did
when we flung into every room,
knocking things all over with our elbows.

If you cover my eyes, I will never notice these things.
I will be shaded from the wailing and tax collectors.
I will be spared all the sadness I could have seen.

You will always find me in the red petals of waterfalls,
in the red coxcomb of the rooster throwing his warnings,
in the accidental blood on the linen when you bite your lip,
in the red barn where a cow pleads to be milked dry,
in the thrasher as it tosses tear drops of red clay,
in your own red eyes from the emptiness of your bed.

The Harmony of the Found

> "Oh, let me remember you as you were before you existed."
> —Pablo Neruda

There was tension when the wind brought dust.
I had almost given up with sweeping.

Each day was irreconcilable with the next.
In the mirror, I was older than I remembered.

There was a rift between what I believed
and what I knew. But now, singing was returning.

What could cause this aria? It is simple:
someone has entered my life

as if it was a door, and they held the secret key.
I was not expecting this to ever happen again.

I had made the moon feel my tension,
and I had the trees clash with the land.

I was used to quarreling with my failures;
then, the singing came:

in the chorus of shifting colors;
in the response from the baker's oven;

singing was in the arrangement of rosebuds.
What I had been missing had been found:

it was as simple as dissension among politicians;
it was as common as friction when hands warm themselves;

it was effortless when I finally breathed into your neck,
smelling the remembrance of love. There the missing was.

Song of the Bottomless Lament

(Based on the poems of Neruda and Lorca)

1.

The days bring dust to my doorsteps
and no one else's doorstep.
I can sweep fruitlessly and never clean enough.
I might as well gnaw on my bruised knuckles.

I live in a village of despair.

The winds knock ruthlessly on our locked doors,
demanding what they cannot have
and refusing to turn away to leave us alone.

The women cry immense dryness.
Their lips are chapped and bleed white carnation petals.
When they tilt their heads in their old, knowing ways,
their bodies portray more than innocence or guilt.

Men who should know better, do not.
Men who should be ashamed of their failure
do not admit willingly to such things and deny them.
They move about as if nothing was wrong with the way things are.

There is not any absolution for such a place.
Someone should do something about this before it is too late.

Silence is a careful man full of frantic stillness.
Silence hangs in the dust.
It sneaks pass the barriers, sliding under skirts.
Silence dwells in the man dragging his feet in shame.

2.

I see one of those men.
He hates to admit it. But there he walks,
pocketing shame and regret.

He walks in dust, smothering words.
The lament means nothing to him.
He can go around ignoring it.
He can ignore what he wants without pity.

However, another part of him,
sobs endlessly and piteously
for the loss of himself,
for his unwillingness to do any different.

He has condoned what he knows
and accepts the unacceptable.

He brushes his teeth with this humiliation,
dresses himself with embarrassment.

If he removes his work-boots and finds blisters,
it will be of his own doing.
If he spits out disgust and does not wipe himself,
then he deserves to be treated with disgust.

So, if he must speak, he must clear his voice
like he had swallowed polluted waters.
He must denounce loudly his silent lament.
He must shout as if loosening gales of crows.

3.

If a lament does not go deep enough,
then it is not a lament at all.
If the lament does not burst out of a man in a torrent,
then it is not a lament at all.

If men do nothing to improve the world,
then the lament is not lament at all.
If he thinks they should do nothing.
then do nothing—and lament not at all.

If, on the other hand,
men find lament is a sharp stick,
they must respond.

If nothing else, break the lament.

The Transitory World

*

All day, begonia petals number across fields
as the sky trembles behind its gauze screen.
At the edge of a mountain, a scarlet bird
dips into a lost stream, then tries to escape
the lack of sound in its own frightened heart.
Now, there will be no love poems
between sheets, whispering and cooing.

I keep thinking of you, even when you've gone.

All day, all night, into the forever,
birds surge in air, mountainous formations of birds—
escaping, returning, shouting:
Beloved, beloved, hear me!

When one has a secret lover, it can be like this.

*

Each year turns into a hundred poems of Love
never sent, in fear of rejection.
Each day, we wait for what never arrives.

Love is an empty boat, drifting away,
distant.
Someone else might not see it—but not me.

If only I was the water,
I would have something,
but I have the instead.

*

An evening bell rings for monks—
incense in quiet air.

What separates us from the world?
I can only drink your distance.

Soon, there will be parting-sorrow.
But for now, there are the evening bells.

*

More mist than lover,
I have left the garden of troubled nights,
entered every room of myself, shaking dust,
calling your name.

But you could not answer.

Willow trees keep everything out of sight.
They do not hide tears falling as your hairpins.

I called out to you—and loons responded.
The sun traveled from the west
to when we first found each other.

There are two types of longing:

one is the desire for togetherness,
where our shoes are next to each other
trying to mate;

the other is the fierce loneliness,
when one journeys onward,
leaving the other—
wishing for the return to togetherness:

a river of Love poems;
a hundred suns; a toss of begonia petals,
boats moving slow; lovers holding hands;
birds spiraling air;
the sky weeping shooting stars.

from
COMING HOME CELEBRATION

FutureCycle Press, 2019

Coming Home Celebration

(An expression for a funeral)

The mourners peer into the face of death
and recall their own tremendous loss.
Then time shrinks with mercy.

He is home now.

These greeters only touch the robes
of death and feel it is contagious.

This is our third visitation in a short time,
different ways of mourning and accepting:
three different ways to journey,
be greeted, three celebrations of the unknown;
very humbling. The body in the casket
is not there anymore, the ashes in the can
are not present anymore, the words
we have and do not have, are never enough.
Our tears are shaped like calla lilies.

Outside, a homeless man holds a sign
reminding everyone how far we can fall
from grace, from favor, forgotten
and alone.
Visitations of memories flush by
rapid as sparrows. We live to witness death.

We go home after the wake, after breaking bread
and passing stories about the dead person,
feeding on these seeds. We pass the callas
to remind us of resurrection and forgiveness.
We pass the man begging and offer nothing,
and we are found wanting. Where is his home?
Where do the sparrows go when no one is looking?
Where do calla lilies go when they drop all petals?

People look into the casket and see themselves.
When they go to sit for the service,
they should be asking, *who do we serve?*

But those words are not much more
than homeless sparrows, or altars of white lilies:
all pretty to look at, all reassuring to hear,
all transitory, short-lived, dying before completed.

This Is What We Cannot See

Everywhere between heaven and earth is fragile.
Fear could tendril like vines, if we let it.
It is too easy to surrender, too comfortable
to be depressed; harder to transmute
into particles of light when expressing love,
but that is what is needed. All of this earth-swell,
this cadence of morning and evening flow,
is just a rehearsal for whatever is next in life.

All perceptions are immediate
when they should be re-evaluated
for the totality of the experience,
otherwise, we are short-changing ourselves.

Today, the door of dreams opened
and a woman walked into the unknown
just to know it.

Wooden Bench

1.

She leads him through mist to a wooden bench.
Sit down; I have something to tell you.

He knows that this cannot be good.
He feels the bench although he does not remember sitting.
He notices that none of the birds are making any sounds.
The silence is awkward, and time stopped like deer.
He knows that this cannot be good.

He listens as urgent as the deer ready to sprint.
The hairs on his arms are on the edge of fear.
No, this is not going to be good.
He can tell. He can tell by the tone of her voice.

He wonders how long he had been sitting.
Waiting for bad news always takes longer than good news.
The world is focused and out of focus.
This is definitely not good. Not by anyone's standards.

He knows what is coming next.
He does not want to hear it.
It is going to be really bad. He knows it.
He knows it like the trees know sparrow nests.

Here it comes.

2.

She kicks off her shoes. She wants to feel the grass.
She rubs her feet into it until her soles turn green.
Her feet shift, nervous.
She cannot look directly into his eyes.

He knows what is coming.
He waits for her to say it.
He holds on like it will be the last time.
He does not want to let go.

Letting go could mean a separation.
He does not want that to happen.
He holds on.
Some news just need time.

He notices her shoes.
They are between him and the distance
near the top of the bench.
She tells him the terminal news.

     3.

In the hospital, she shrinks in his arms.
I am afraid.

What can he say to that?

She has slipped off the hospital slippers.
Her feet are green.

He admits: *Me too.*

Afterwards, the nurse in hospital greens
leads him away. He sits on a bench.
He feels the hard wood later, much later.
He thinks: *this is not good.*

     4.

Afterwards, he realizes she is dead,
been dead for weeks now.
The memory of her visiting him on a bench
was not real. But the bench, her hand, the rest,

it felt so real.

A Clear Voice Singing

The air warms this late in the day. Geese gather
and practice formations—off and on, circle, fall—
breath in the breathlessness. The sun is a single car
light arriving over the rise of horizon,
behind schedule, trying to make up time.

Every moment becomes difficult. We see it
coming with that slowed-down hesitant sun.
Black shapes of geese overhead are practicing
and readying. All that work is ending.

We trade season for season, resolved
in the fact we cannot control any of this—
not one struggle of it. When we lose control,
we have acknowledged and accepted
what is ours and what is not. When we die,
we let go of all responsibility, all chores,
all conflict, all breath and breathlessness.

Closing the Cabin

Each year, he would close the summer cabin—
this would be the last time he would process
the procedure for laying it to rest. Now, he knew,
this would be his last time—
his last reflection on the lake surface,
a final tip of oar leaving water.

He tugged the lumbering canoe up shore,
flipped it over, rubbed off the moss,
and sunbaked the canoe for wintering.

He could feel the last days coming—
the last fling at the cabin.
He did not fear it; just wondered at it,
as though studying a butterfly up close
to see through its waxy wings.

This would be the last scent of pine; the knock
of woodpecker; a last kingfisher's snaring trout
and lifting its rainbow molecules of water droplets.
What would the next life be like?

Or would he have summers still?
What would he witness?
Would it be true? Would it be elusive or effervescent?
Would it resonate?
Would he attest to the stillness, the immensity
and intensity of silence? There were sounds
so ingrained, he could hear them even in the next world.
Would there be more?

He had been able to hear the pine needles
singing in stilled wind.
Would there be more? Was there more? Was this it?

Would the latch on the screen be it, or the repair of a screen?
Would it be the ice chest draining water? Would the world
continue to sigh? He looked at the roof tile—
how it gathered leaves, desperately, not letting go.
But unlike this busy world, he was ready to let go.

He boarded the window from the crows,
sank his toes into the gravel,
held each image like the pictures he never took
and always promised he would—and if he had,
would he have put them in a photograph album?
Who would turn the page asking what that was?
Mostly, would he remember?

Already, the epileptic moon stumbled across the night—
time moved too quickly; what remained of his life
was in the process of going—what did he have for it?

A maple leaf scooted across hard ground,
making a scraping sound, taking the quiet with it.
He checked the scene one last time, just once more—
then opened his car door, a dome light going on.
His hand was inside the light, while the rest of his body
was still entering into the car with a curling motion
of settling behind the steering wheel. It was too late
to be leaving—regret held him back—
clouds were pulling through empty fall branches
looking too much like his dead wife's hair.

A Letter Explaining Death

I am at a better place now
where the room does not darken at sundown,
where shrimp boats lower nets of light,
where the shoals never rise into fists,
where the beach is never crowded
and the lighthouse beacon swings over the land
casting light in all directions,
where the rocking chair has a cushion
as I knit from endless yellow skeins of yarn,
where everything reminds me of postcards,
where a dirt road ambles by the front picket fence
lined with pansies and yellow irises,
where they still deliver bottles of milk,
where no one needs to lock the door,
where everyone smiles
carrying buckets of conversation,
where no one grows tired of giving greetings,
where neighbors want to invite you to visit
to taste homemade cookies still warm,
where the hard work never begins or ends.

On a clear day, I can see you across the fields
in the kitchen baking pies,
worrying the dough with your fists,
the apples peeled as wet eyes, the apron
smudged with flour, a dress on the line
flapping as it waves hello.

I know your life is a poem needing revision.
Take each word in your life and shake it
as cinnamon.
When you do this, I know your pain
as clear as the timer on the oven,
or the apple peels in the basket,
or the sugar on your cheeks,
or the warmth of the kitchen
as you bake as if your life depended on it.

Slow down. Enjoy that comfort.
I am there with you, reciting the recipe.
I am with you setting the temperature.
When you slice that pie, I will help you with the knife.
When the dishes need cleaning, leave them for me.
Leave them for tomorrow. Go into the living room.
Rest.

At night, turn out the light,
hold memory like you held me
when I was afraid of the dark.
Think about the fact that it is always light here
and there is no more darkness to fear.

For My First Wife Who Died on a Late August Day Much Like Today

I tried to reassemble her, like building a house of cards,
but sections kept crumbling, like her mind.

Snow was in her words, never settling on anything.
Snow accumulated in the hem of my heart.

That's the thing about snow. It never lasts,
and when it's gone, it comes back when you least need it.

There is no comfort in this. I know. I tucked her
in a comforter to her chin. Her feeble smile

haphazardly appeared. What did she see,
when nothing she could remember?

She went to that place where snow goes.
What did she take along with her?

She did not recognize me, and it did not matter.
I have been shoveling ever since, although nothing stays.

Coming From a Dark County

There are no fittings of silence, no secrets
in stones, huge as doors.
I find a solemn weariness to the dark.
In a shattered world, the birds cannot sing
without being shot.

Leave the forsaken behind.
Do not look back. The past is burning.

A shade is pulled where secrets hide.

Someone swings a lantern in the fields
like a single firefly.
Huge stones open like fresh-dug graves.

A crow sound flushes the woods.

A sorrel tilt its head towards that disappearance,
anticipating a week of tremendous losses.

The horizon of wind has overtaken breath.
Bitterness extends to the man in the yard
until his anger takes a turn for the worse.

Crows Are Not Afraid to Talk About Death

They pull apart the sinew of conversation
to get to the marrow of life-and-death situations.
They have a one-track mind.
They know autopsy and recycling;
the sun's blanched bones;
the anatomy of heatstroke; and failed brakes.

They mock everything,
knowing miracles come their way—
a thump here, a slash there.

They can care less
about the complexity of the universe,
unless it includes death;
and then they will begin chattering,
incessant and mimicking,
mocking short-lived things.

They are not concerned with the weather,
or sports, or cracked asphalt, or tomato worms.
To crows, there is little to be gained
by those useless concerns.

They repeat variations of words about death,
looking up a thesaurus for more words to chew on.

I tell them—*hush.*

They laugh. They laugh black raindrops,
falling backwards with incredulous cackling,
snorting so hard, they almost choke on their meal.
They snicker, clicking black tongues.

Loss

I am still in that place of sadness
attentive to any sound returning

if I had known
the doors stayed open this long
I would have brought more words

more kindness

some people prefer quiet moments
of reflection

but there is more noise than I expected
emitting from the center of my heart
echoing out into the emptiness
for any return message

from
THE TEMPORARY WORLD

Blue Light Press, 2019
(Recipient of the Blue Light Press Award)

Before Words

1.

Before words, days had no meaning.
We could draw antelopes leaping energy off cliffs.

We could go in any direction because no boundaries existed.
Yellow mustard days were within reach.

There was no reason to want anything
in the dawning of words.

2.

Somebody wanted more—

more flint; more ripe raspberries;
more land someone else had—

to get more, they forged words
for hunting or berries
or bad weather or danger.

3.

Language was created
when a man carved a naked woman
with enlarged breasts
on a mastodon's ivory
and still had no words
to express his feelings.

Even when he owned words,
he never could explain his feelings
any more than he could rip the moon
out of the midnight sky
or stop that emptying feeling in his heart.

So, when a woman walked away,
her breasts swaying,
it left him wondering
what he should have said,
how comforting were those breasts
whenever he snuggled against them,
how her face in the moonlight calmed him,
how her body was smooth as the bone
he was carving—

stroking the memory-idol of her body,
reclaiming the calm of turtle-wind.

4.

Language was created
when a woman gave birth,
pushing a child out

of the cave of her body—

a baby swimming out
into the waiting hands
of a female shaman
fingering an amulet of bloodstone
evoking visions
to name the child.

5.

Men conspired then
to own all of the mysteries,

hunting the night for answers,
naming the sun, a male god.

6.

God tossed out words
from his velvet mouth:

raindrops

men caught them all.

Before Letters

1.

Before eels swam in electric water,
before words were written,
a man walked in the Alps,
wearing deerskin boots,
searching for missing sheep
in wind howling like hungry wolves.

A sudden avalanche took him and his screams away.

2.

When someone found the frozen, ancient body.
thousands of centuries later,
it looked as if he had been trying to write something
with the sewing needle
used to mend his handmade boots.

3.

Words roam loose—
fitting all descriptions,
escaping boundaries of this page,
taking the odor of printing presses
and the touch of laughter.

4.

Words are unruly, disobedient,
sticking their tongues out.

Words gather as a distrustful crowd,
following us down gloomy passageways.

Our hearts are loud and struggling,
but words do not want to listen.

Words pick out meaning
as the nocturnal insect of death.

Before Numbers

  1.

before numbers
the world was within sight
we could walk to the border
and there was no edge
marking beginning or end

we never knew how far
or close we were to disaster

never knew heights or depths
never knew our limits

numbers changed the calculations

  2.

the world was simpler then
you traded objects

a man could build his own house
with rough hands
and measure with his feet

anything more
or less
anywhere further beyond walking
beyond sight
was beyond wanting

  3.

someone decided standard numbers
were necessary to know
how many or how few or
how much or how little
or how they lived without numbers

someone wanted imaginary numbers
someone wanted more
someone was counting on it

  4.

after numbers were assigned
man discovered he really did not want
the number of problems

and even zero
had value

5.

a pyramid of decimals greets me at the door
fractions ride barrels over Niagara Falls
clouds practice long-division, problems multiply
algebra is as seasonal as blueberries
gravity plops newspapers to my doorstep
a whirlwind of minus signs darkens
the vanishing-point sky
numbers are juggled by accountants

6.

one is an open door

two makes a Blues number
when your lover becomes a two-timer

the grocery store scales are weightless
until filled
by three artichokes at the counter

four lost letters arrive
they do not belong to me
they do not belong to this address
I break them open like eggs

five wooly mammoths trumpet loudly
their wet fur stinks of tundra
they buy electric shavers
and breath mints
they pay with six gold doubloons

7.

on my seventeenth year
a 65 cherry-red Chevy pulls up
taking me past my 11 o'clock curfew
burning all four rubbers

if you gave me ten rules
I'd break them into 57 pieces

gravity cannot hold a teenager
that has any number of excuses
and a fake ID

8.

now age limits me
miles abuse my face
gravity keeps me nine to five
a regular guy
listing rules
for my teenage son
knowing full well
he'll break them all
plus some extra ones
like a combination lock

I can count on it

Letter

A half-mad letter was in my pocket all day
reminding me
things were not going well.
Not at all.

In the amount of removed light,
it sent distraught messages
no one wanted to hear.

Its letters were moving around in my pocket,
exploring
how things should always be good,
but they never are.

I wanted the blueprint of memories.

During a Conversation of Many Voices

Some were carried undertow
into a drowning.
The distant shore was elusive.

Some were taken away—stiff currents;
lightning striking water,
churning them into blood.
Still, no one noticed.

The roar was overcoming. Seagulls flew out
of the harbors of our arms,
still
no one noticed the floundering.

Out of the drenching,
wearing slickers,
waving lanterns, no shore in sight,
no one noticed
how everyone's mouths
opened, closed,
like fish on land.

I kept the oars to myself.

Only dark clouds opened their hands
and let go.

Air

I could not tell you then how close you were to death, blue as a stone,
how chickadees stopped their tormenting love long enough
to feel pity, how silence sat in a rocking chair, holding the pulse
of a blue vein, looking for some faint sigh of light. I could not tell you then,
for I needed you to fight back, my rescue breathing had failed.

I cracked your ribs like walnut shells, forcing space to push out
the Nothingness inhabiting you, section by section, occupying
what should be, by rights, yours.

I could not tell you over the coldness,
the shifting iceberg in your bones, that I was losing you.
You had to find your own way back.

I waved frantically, *this way.*
I could not tell you, because you could not hear.

You were not here. You were headed to the *Elsewhere.*
My training was failing both of us; and you were heading
towards that more insistent calling. All I was holding
was the stone of your life.

They told me I had done everything. I had been at it for hours.
I worked while you were dead. This was no comfort.
I saw you in the blue moon, the unmoving rocking chair,
the air you never had, the coldness of summer at noon,
bones cracking like ribs, the light on a walnut shell.

Walking into Remembrance

1.

My life was a waning moon, where belief comes and goes.

Sounds of waterfalls change.
Clouds are eternal islands always transforming.
Why not me?

Heavy dew-fall of plums; a shadow at noon,
a distance where the missing are more interesting
than the found.

2.

A garden without a coat, shivers loose feeding birds.
Birds are erased and reappear, but with new colors.

Stars spill out of chrysanthemums as if from jars.
Clouds are burning in exhausted shade.

The world is in turmoil thinking you might be gone someday.
Don't walk so far into memory you can't come back.

Glass Walls Do Not a Barrier Make

Based on *Open Box 3,* by Joel Haber

Put a glass wall to hide the truth; you can still see it.
Tear out the windows like black eyes, empty our sockets;
we are not blind to our situation.
Prop up the sides of our house and declare it safe;
it will fall on us with the next light wind.
Chain the glass to poles, thinking it will stop winds;
the winds will simply cross over and topple us.

The island can rise up into the air, but it takes more
to help an island to repair itself, takes more
for people to pick up the splinters. Open a box,
and misery will go with the winds, perhaps, to you,
and if you wake up devastated, you will understand.

If you want to do something useful, do it quickly.
Otherwise, do not pretend my house is invisible,
when it can be seen clearly behind a glass wall.
Do not pretend my house has chairs and walls,
do not mistake the broken wood scattered everywhere
as edible or practical for repairs.

Certainly, do not think this shows just a diorama
representing the worse of conditions.
Our lives are torn, blackened refugees.

As the wind goes, so too the sand.

Weightless as Blossoms in Wind

in a field of white lit lanterns
petals fall like white moths
taking fragrance with them

the amazing is always on the other side of the door
you need to pry it open and peer inside

Some Days

I can imagine the world without me.
It troubles me, this knowledge,
the truth of what it means.

For the certainty of days
and the certainty of nights,
there are continuous moments.

Sometimes, I imagine you without me—
and that too troubles me—so much time lost between us,
so many times, when we could have said one last goodbye.

How, too, I think, endlessly,
the heart continues
and somehow it mends itself.

If there is comfort in this, let it remain.
If it troubles you, let it go.

Improvisations in Darkness

1.

The delineation from lamp,
circuitous
around a corner, into
a dark room, narrowing
into lost light,
disappearing—
one reality
into another.

Going into the unknown,
expect surprises.

2.

Going from dark
into darker,
there is always
ambient light—

rain
against windows:
soft, hard,
then noticing

it's gone.

3.

In Total Darkness,
you develop a sense
of where things are.

You do not need to see them.
You know their shape,
density, their dark purpose,
knowing how to avoid them
using radar.

If only
this worked in relationships,
there would be no failure,

we'd all know what to do,
who to avoid,
what to say, when to say it
instead of blurting
the first thing

coming to the tip of our tongue
with no way
to reel it back in.

     4.

In Total Darkness
there is no such thing
as darkness.

The lack of light,
is the lack of imagination.

True blindness
is not seeing things
for themselves.

We do this in first love.

Light comes on.
We realize we made a mistake,
an error in judgment,
darkness floods our hearts,
switches off our brains,
drains blood from our veins.

Blindness continues
even after knowing the facts.

     5.

In Total Darkness
we learn to use other senses,
the ones less traveled—

pinpricks of awareness,
air against skin,

hair on our arms, rising
like antennas.

Emerge into light
with the same, tentative steps.

     6.

When doubting in shadows
remember
first buds—
blue Johnny-jump-ups,

white fawn lilies,
pink Chinese hellebore,
crepe-paper Oriental poppy.

Under last year's leaves,
white, bell-shaped
snowdrops uncurl,
first and foremost.

What comes, goes—

but memory, ah, memory
curls out of itself.

7.

Memory comes,
and unfortunately,
goes
when needed most.
Age removes it,
giving instead forgetfulness,

Why can't memory be
a buttercup
we held to our chins
when we were children
to see who liked butter?

This Buttercup Memory
would show
who remembers
what is necessary
and forgets
what needs forgiving.

8.

This is for my mother,
heading into Alzheimer's
like it was a destination,
a one-way, no exit strategy,
all the others
hopelessly lost,
as everything disappears,
nothing remaining.

I might be coming your way.

9.

Until then,
I grab onto fistfuls of light,
keep them in a drawer,
write flames of memory,
turn darkness into origami,
my chin yellow
from holding a buttercup.

The opposite of loss is finding.

from
UNFOLDING OF LOVE

WIPF and Stock Publishers, 2020

In the Beginning We Tumble into Light

In the beginning we tumble into Light.
We communicate in basic sounds
to express our needs. We need light,
sleep, and nourishment. Our frailness
makes tenderness and care possible.
Our imprint of wailing need is constant
and dependent. This is never forgotten,
yet outgrown. Our small reaching arms
and tracking eyes test what sounds
evoke and which are ignored.
Sound is foreign and learned, mimicked
and memorized, cause and effect passed
from child to parent, sharing common need.
From soundlessness to combining sounds,
making engagement, words are both archeology
and expansion. Communication is the beginning
of misunderstanding. We are embodied in language.

It is so hard to talk with You.
Your words engaged my beginnings.
It should be easy as light and sound.
We should start with endlessly talking,
never running out of things to say or share,
or questioning, fishing for answers in shallow streams.
Let it always be this easy. It is easy
as finding secrets in an acorn among the wordlessness.

Silence waits to speak,
from the beginning, when all things were said.
I am on the ledge of awe.

Tender Music

I did not expect this sky to be talking,
although its blue lips were moving over the fields
like a woman asking permission.

Someone needs to listen. Someone
needs to bundle days
before they completely unravel.

Blue snow wavers, obliterating this world,
its trees, that river and its dragging
of debris like a silence of birds.

Someone needs to be tender music.
The world waits for us
to step into what we've never seen.

Swan

In spite of its soundlessness,
the male trumpet swan chases the mallards,
making itself larger than the fear
flying out of the mallards' hearts.

The Spirit Moving the Silence

we discern by listening inside that movement
to hear what is not spoken
but felt

nothing seems to be there
then a presence seeps in

no one is there to whisper the words
although it resides as memory
of water and birth
a song that never ends

we are distracted when we hear it
suddenly a dark room has light

what do you hear

a sound less than ice forming
or a butterfly opening its wings

what do you hear

I see your head turning towards the words
going quiet
trying to focus on the source
and what it is saying

I hear that voice too
it is urging *listen*

listen

Lead Me

teach me how to enter a deeper silence
hover inside
reassure me
whatever is troubling me
will pass

so much to handle

I want all my problems
to launch off
like an armada of wintering geese
announcing their departure

I want to hear
within the silence
I want to harvest those words

teach me to how to stay quiet

let the words inside the silence
be lilac spray

April 17

It's April. It's snowing—again.
And, again, flowers close.

Snow is a cruel joke.

The world is speechless,
disappointed—
all this unfulfilled desire!
It is April, after all.
It's not supposed to be like this—

white, cold shock,
purpose driven away—

this peculiar weather,
this unevenness,
this lack of rapture.

It's our turn,
insist the purple crocuses.

Snow returns, anyway,
any way it can.

Death can happen at any time.

We can only sing our way forward.
The journey is long,
and the length varies
depending on each of us,

and when we get to the end,
tired, forlorn,
we will brighten up,
at last, and open
like spring flowers.

Lamentation for a Natural World

For years, the box elder has wrestled the wind,
the damp nights, the stars
grazing the meadows of the endless horizon,
the snow creeping up, the frost
speckled finger markings.

I wish I could say I could tolerate the winter,

but I have to go inside,
check the thermostat a couple of times,
wrap a comforter around my shoulders,
shiver out the deep chill.

The wind whines like a child
waking with night terrors.

I know the song of loneliness when I hear it.

That music settles in differently
than my body trying to generate heat.
Each recollection, each storage
of lost body heat, co-mingles like branches
in fierce wind, shuttering. Each star
is vaguely behind cold
meadows of clouds, snow sneaking in,
offering no comfort, no solace,
no rest from nightmares,
no matter how tightly I grip the blanket,
no matter what song I sing to myself
to keep the sadness from entering me,
a deep and sullen chill.

On a Starry Night

Van Gogh entered that quiet place—
the one where fireflies gathered
in communion. That one area
bounding with grasshoppers in his face
as Presence. He knew he was *there*
at the epicenter of released joy,
where the worrisome day and concerns
fragmented into powder
smaller than yellow pollen.

Above his brown straw hat,
galaxies spiraled as ballerinas—
such fearless Light—God turned his breath
into brushstrokes—Vincent felt his body
molding like bread dough,
weariness splattered out of him.

There was no edge between the horizon
and sky and God. He did not need windows
to see clearly anymore.

This Is What Happens When Your Name Is Called and You Missed Your Turn

God was thumbing through
the ledger of names
accidentally touched mine

a sea came
into my second-floor room
luminous and melting the walls

there was a canoe of thorns
no paddles
but a written invitation

I never suspected this would happen
but in a world full of momentary seconds
I floated past the moon

I forgot to write down all I saw
it was like midday
when no one knows when it is here

the next I knew
I had circled back to my body
covered with spiraling universes

this all happened the same day
God created the idea of God
and someone else tried to take the idea away.

Love Is Never Far from Us

Love, perhaps, is not far from us,
yet it seems so far away;
we are overwhelmed with loss.

If we believe (for our belief is false)
love is gone forever, it betrays—
love, perhaps, is not far from us.

Love is never far away. Love is never lost.
It is with us every day.
We are overwhelmed with loss.

Small moments remind us what's false.
Love comes again, today and today.
Love, perhaps, is not far from us;

maybe, the sadness is just across.
We never know completely what to say,
we are overwhelmed with loss.

We try to hold on and let go at all costs.
Sometimes, love comes unexpectedly.
Love, perhaps, is not far from us—
we are overwhelmed with loss.

Presence

a sparrow landed on a branch,
barely moving the limb
with its light heartfelt song

this can be a quiet world
even when there is a song
moving in a tall tree

even if the melody hooks into my heart
this can be a quiet place
stirring from branch to fence to sky

this can be such a quiet
quiet
world we live in

when the sparrow goes away
it takes its song with it
this world can be a silent place

How Leaves Form

at the tip of each branch
a green hope buds
a whisper

both stillness and

Presence

unfolding

a sluggish wintered soul
readying to appear
a sleeper

slowly stirring
when it opens from within
all secrets rush out
green words

What the Soundlessness Is Telling Us

The absence of sound
creates the presence of amplified noises
so minuscule, we cannot hear them—

a baby sighs in an upstairs bedroom,
a first-time parent rushes
to check to make certain the baby is alright;

or a bat, glides after mosquitoes; or
maple sap surges into syrup; or chalk
scribbles on a blackboard.

Folding the laundry, I made the neat creases,
sighing a quiet memory into each piece,
the day after my first wife died.

Wakening

The intensity of love, suggested Wallace Stevens,
that is what will be missing—*that* quickness! The *more,*
more, more we feel while in love. Birds cascading
like melodies! *That,* that is what is absent: the world
opening a book of infinite pages, fully felt. Our hopes
and barriers are the spine holding us together.
We never know what to expect, but we're willing
to risk it together. We waken to the sharp focus
of this world we never noticed before, and it is blindly
present, moving through this landscape.
We can almost touch the abstract shape of love.

Some people sigh for the lack of love;
some take for granted the presence of love;
some, the lucky ones, waken to gladness of love,
holding that quickening like liquid mercury,
like a bird trembling in their hands.

I left the bed with my wife still sleeping
bundled in blankets, the memory of her
from last night shifting through my spine;

I cover her again, kiss her exposed head, watch
her snuggle into the curve of love. I am fortunate
to know she was what was missing in my life,
intensely, yellow light everywhere, absolute and widening.

Not Yet

All plants tremble in the fall sadness. Not yet.
Not yet. This way, that way, thrashing in gusts,
flinging loose leaves and petals, piece
by exotic-green changing piece. Not yet; please,
not yet. Rough tastes of wind pluck the plants apart,
making liver spots, rustic burnt sienna, yellow
jaundice, wrinkled. Not yet. No, not yet.
The fallen scuttle, settle, exhausted, then tremble
in strangling wind, calm down yet again.
Yet again, not yet. Every winter some might liquify.
Every snowfall, branches scold the season
for ravishing every leaf this way and that.

I know, I know, not yet. Yet, we all end eventually.
We all head towards a home, this way, that,
trembling in sadness with exhausted breath,
not yet, not yet. I know my settling is coming,
spiraling downwards like leaves, that way, this,
and I am thrashing and loosening from this world
towards—not yet! Not yet, I am not falling, not yet.
I am not taken yet by the wind, this way, that way,
seasons leaf by, pages of ravished endings.

At the Beginning

There was a time, when the stars reached down
to lift us up—but those days of actual salvation
abandoned those who ignored the stars.
When told to go somewhere,
people went elsewhere.
Their wandering continued long after
the wanderlust flamed out.

Nothing that was made was made to last.
There was no language that included Others.
So, they left out strangers.
Nothing caught anyone's attention;
nothing that meant some kind of connection.

Which brings us to here. Not exactly
where we expected to be.
The world is still being created,
refined, re-imagined. All the busy activity
goes on with or without us, like dreams
other people have. We want to be a part,
and also, to be standing aside, observing,
feeling either important or unworthy.

This is when we go still,

overwhelmed with the lack of control
we have over outcomes. Everything we try
can find its own direction, even if
it's looping back into the way we were before.

I am telling you some message
without understanding, exactly,
what you will do with the information.

The Midday Nap

Based on the painting by Vincent Van Gogh, 1889

Not so fast, world. Not so fast. There will be time
for things both pleasurable and work
so tiring, your arms are ropes of pain.

We need to find that moment when things rest
in a field of cut hay, under a triangle shade,
far from the fall harvest, far from exhaustion.

I have learned to take these short siestas,
while the sun plods like a horse never stopping.
A few minutes are all I need.

I am more with the shadows than not. I squint
under a straw hat into what needs to be done.
These are seasons of endless roped haystacks.

I shrug muscles already feeling the swinging scythe.
Already gone to where things are never interrupted.
Gone like peaches canned. Or fences mended and breaking.

What is held? The sky is yellow felled grains.
It always will be planted and harvest again.
Always will be this way. Always was.

There will always be couples resting in shade.
They will work until the day is bundled as the hay,
where love is always beginning and ending.

from
HARVEST TIME

Deerbrook Editions, 2020

The Sounds Water Makes

Grandmother hated the rusty click-clack whoosh
metallic sound of the kitchen hand pump,
preferring I'd go out: *Fetch a wooden bucket*
of water from the well.

I'd creak-creak the pulley rope
until I'd feel the bucket slap-bottom-touch the water,
go slower, sensing it sink-fill, then
tug-yanked up into sunlight, a slushing bucket,
fetched it back.

Water tasted different when from a bucket
or the hand-pump or metal ladle at the well.
I never understood how the texture and flavor changed.

All I knew was Grandma hated the fancy hand pump,
choosing the old Amish, sensible ways,
without gadgets and gizmos. She desired a world
waking up to hardness of life, as loose
as water. But the rest of the world was moving
in a blur she'd never understand, leaving her behind,
set in her ways, her bones too old and stubborn
for there to be any other way than plain-spoke,
careful with words, listening before speaking,

She wanted a time when water was water,
and sky clung fiercely to the land.
She declared, "You can keep your ways."

I was too afraid to ask her what she was going to do
with all that water. I went softly back outside,
floors screech-scratching behind me
like a rope being lowered into the deepest well.

Laundry Hanging Day

She knows it is probably the last day
to hang laundry, as long as the weather holds.
The season is thinning. The days are colder.
She studies the cloud cover blocking the sun,
willing the clouds out of the way. She pins
hope. The clothes are heavy with water,
so she twists them out. That will have to do.
She is tempting the rain; she knows it,
but it'd be worth it to have pine scent
in the sheets when she goes to sleep.

The fabric will remember the trees
and woodpeckers and the small,
sensitive ferns closing when touched.

She looks to the clouds for a sign,
any sign. Will it rain? Will it clear up?
She tries willing the clouds into moving.
She hums like a bee. She hears her husband
hammering loose shingles before winter sets in.
The wooly bear caterpillar was as fat as her thumb:
a true sign the snow will last as long as her laundry line.

Will the weather hold just a little bit longer?
Geese spread sheets in the sky.

Perhaps, the day will remain perfect, just for her:
unspoiled, unsoiled, dry to the touch. Please,
she prays, let something be perfect.

Working on My Grandparents' Farm

I'd get my hand slapped if I ate without praying first;
or scolded if I didn't spin wool thin as forgiveness.
Grandmother warned me, life wouldn't be easy.
I'd be out before the roosters woke,
rain or shine or extreme punishing heat.
Clouds of swallowtail butterflies
would swish out of the fields
as dogs rounded up the sheep.

Grandfather seldom talked. His silence
was a different language: one of intense concentration
and repetition to get what needed to be done.
We'd work hand-in-hand, never speaking,
and the lessons I was learning weren't in a book.
Roosters set their clocks by us. His approval was a smile,
a sideways glance to make sure I got it right.
I'd hammer horseshoes on an anvil, sparking sunbreak,
or tan leather until it was smooth as butterfly wings
or split firewood, deep center, one blow, evenly,
or scythe with a swoosh-swing in a golfer's stance.
Swallowtails would spin up in air
into storm clouds, as if chased by dogs.

I'd work like a hound in the dog days when the earth steamed,
so sultry and tormented all I wanted to do was go limp.
Yet I'd work twice as hard. And I'd get little rewards:
Grandfather no longer demonstrating,
but trusting I'd do it right,
or Grandmother smiling slowly
when I made a blanket on a loom, shooting the shuttle
though with a *snap.*

Knowing the Answers

cows lowing in narrow stalls
moving shoulders
remembering repetition and anticipation
the bead of last night's rain
shuddering on the eve
eyes holding the reflection
of moon or memory
it's hard to tell which

the night is no longer creeping around
giving and taking
sleep

the cows know
we are coming
before we arrive
providing relief

we untie problems
now
like shoelaces
one
knot at a time

Cow Barn

Thought I'd never escaped that smell
of urine and straw. It seeped in my skin
as much as the muck I raked and hosed.
Was in more places than I could tell.
Leaned on the air. Squirted like milk
in buckets. No cleaning eliminated it.
My brother's bed after-night-wetting smell.
There was nothing glamorous in this work.
At first, it was fun. After a while, it grew old.
From urine-colored sun to when night fell,
it was endless, like a curse, like penance.
Days were squeezed like a cow being milked.
Years later, the smell comes to me in swells
like sea foam. My hands remember milking
the difference between punishment and work,
love and anger, heaven and hell.

Milking

Guernsey cows lug their milk-heavy bodies
on the same worn-down trail
blazed by generations of their ancestors,
knowing not one care in the world,
in the safety of fenced-off pastures.

Moving at the pace of slow rain
drizzling in fits and stops,
nothing disturbs them, after chewing
the grass, drinking from a shallow pond,
swaying tails at biting black flies.

I've been milking, hands yanking pure milk
into metal pails, measuring the offerings,
listening to sloshing against emptiness,
milk filling to the brim, the different tones,
pitches, and completeness of it all.

I will have to decide which one is not producing.
One will have to go. It is the rule of survival, cash,
and costs of feed. None are a pet. None are named.
Otherwise, it will be heard to part with them.
It is unfortunate I have to make this decision.

Their bodies in half-light in morning
are as milk-heavy as a decision. Generations
wearing down a path of ancestors
slow down during rain. They are undisturbed,
as shallow as chewed grass, still being milked.

The Serenade

A cow lies on her side, panting and heaving.
Her tongue slides out uncomfortably.
She wheezes. It won't be long now.
It is a matter of time and discomfort.

Sometimes, this happens
when no one is around to witness—
the earth begins a lullaby.

Here I come to put her out of her misery.
How many times must I do this?

I can do this chore in my sleep. The rifle is heavy.
I pat her head, talking to her in a slow,
careful, reassuring way. What I say
never eases pain,
but I say it anyway, for both of our sakes.

I praise her for the years of milk, for calves.
How many times must I do this—
this kindness—it pains a heart.

The wolves won't get her;
I'll make certain of that.
I pray and sight.
I finish the sentence.

A shot scatters birds for miles—
echoes and rebounds, settles.

I drag the cow using ropes. I am eleven.
The sun is dry with the chorus of locust.
The barrel of the gun is hot, smoking, decisive.

I wish I could walk back in time. I wish
I was in a parallel world. I wish the line
between life and death was longer, more perfect.
I wish suddenness was not a precision drummer.

None of my wishes mean anything.

Dawn still cycles over the fields,
illuminating what I did years ago:
you cannot bury truth.

Now, I write with a fever. The safety is released.
A backfire wakes me up.

Am I revisiting my past on the farm,
or when I worked with wounded in Vietnam?
The world could care less.

But eyes plea: *End it.*

I step in and out of memory like a movie.
Everywhere, there are moments repeating themselves
and I cannot change the past—
the desperate wish for release from suffering.

After every death, there is an intense coda of silence.

Listening to a Handloom

Wool speaks of being sheared and carded.
I'd coaxed it from the sheep
that dogs had barked into a pen.
I'd sharpen the clippers on a whetstone, grinding
until flint-strike spark appeared.

I'd gather pokeweed berries, boil them into dye,
let it dry.

Later, I'd spin the wool on a spindle
into a spool of colored dark-blue thread
for the longitudinal "warp" held still
on a handloom's frame.
The filling yarn was the "woof"
guided by a "shuttle" weaving in and out
like a guided hummingbird
between those threads—that "shedding" portion
when the material creates space for the shuttle
to slip through.

This motion of lifting
and tightening happens automatically
with the "heddle" main frame.

The loom would tell me the story
of labor and patience by doing work the old way.

The loom taught me specialized language.
It wove the story of sacrifice
of the sheep giving wool and me laying low
on a hillside with a single-bolt rifle
protecting them from predators.

I still hear the grass, wet against my face,
a bead of sweat as it trickled down
into my sighted-eye, and a wolf's tail twitch.

Shuttle, shift, *pop*—
the thread as thin as a spider's web,
weaving stories, this work of hands,
patterns zipping through threads of time.

I never talked during any of this work—

I needed concentration to listen:
Be careful, don't miss a stitch.

This story of my life is not over. The *snap*-pull
of the loom makes the thread of light
begin and end each day—soft
whisperings of wool and work-*sigh*.

I have sown this story into the pokeweed night,
each star speaking the language of loom-*snap*.

Silence Has Its Own Language

There are days when I am still ten, following Grandfather
out the back door into the prayer of stars.

There are several ways to know silence—fishing forever
without a bite, your heart moving with a spring steam defrosting;

or mucking the barn, rake scratching wooden floors and straw;
or cat swishing its tail before striking; or goldenrod opening.

Grandfather barely spoke all summer. No need to talk. Words
were wasted, when silent commands and nods worked well.

You can hear more if you listen intently—deer moving at dawn,
inventing silence; or the stillness of heart and hush of breath.

More important, all of earth and stars and silence speak.
You can hear, like a dog ear's perking, everything unsaid.

from
ALL WARS ARE THE SAME WAR

FutureCycle Press, 2022

The Little Gardeners

During WW II, Eerde Castle near Ommen, Netherlands was used by
Quakers to hide over 200 Jewish children (1934-41). The children
described their accounts in *The Little Gardener's Album.*

1.

(All wars are the same war—
only the efficiency of destruction
is different.)

2.

In spite of the circumstances,
moldy bread is quite exceptional.
We grow our own vegetables
in spite of the blackouts.

In spite of the lack of rain,
we gather tears from the smaller children
into a watering can.

3.

Bombers thunder overhead.
We call them harmless mosquitos.

4.

Tomatoes are as big as starvation eyes.
Tomatoes are juicy memories of home.
These circumstances are tiny victories.

We plant in survival
and in spite of the hindrances of squirrels
or fear.

It is good that the Quakers teach silence—
otherwise, we would make noise
waking combat boots.

5.

In spite of the distance
we can hear our parents dying.

6.

Someone says the enemy is near here.
We shall greet them with laughter.
We shall show them our hands holding peppers,
and they will remark,

They are harmless little children.
They will never know where we hid our gold stars.

We planted the stars in the garden.

At night, those stars are string beans heading into sky.
We want to climb them and place more stars
so everyone can see there is no difference
between one star and another.

7.

We wear out the ground with our knees
planting in soil.
The earth speaks a different language
than ours.

Although adults say things look grim,
we see the efforts of cucumbers
climbing the fence
with fingers.

8.

Someone says the school is seven years old.
My brother is the same age.
It is silly to think they have the same mother.
But when I see him
trying to grow into his britches,
and his socks sag in angles
while he fights, uselessly, to straighten them,
I think how careless this world is,
to allow adults to fight over nothing.

9.

They captured our music teacher,
Billy Hilsey—to them, another conquest.

He looked white like a music sheet,
his freckles like notes, as they took him away.
We are told never to speak his name again.

We are commanded
by the man wearing totally black leather.
His sidearm is as polished as his hip boots.
He clicks his heels when he is finished speaking.

He was addressing the houses in the village
as if they had ears. He told the houses
if they saw anyone suspicious
to report to him immediately.

I wait for one of the houses to speak to him.
What exactly would a house say?
Would a house tell this man who to trust?
Would houses confess they know where we are hiding?
Will the doorknobs turn us in?

10.

It is fashionable to hate.
Is that the same way in your part of the world?

Today, we talked about tolerance,
and in the distance was shooting.

When I see myself in a mirror,
is my face really so strange?

Children outside are holding hands
in a ring of silence, praying for love.

11.

On the radio, we hear about cleansing the Earth
of the undesirables. We know it is about us.
We are so small, and the world is so large and angry.

They say we are a hindrance. A pebble
in a shoe. A toothache. Dress rehearsals
for silence when night arrives, marching boots.

They say, *Help is coming, sit tight, wait it out.*
We can hear trucks approaching, men inside
click bullets into chambers.

Someone said Billy Hilsley was shot at close range
for giving the wrong answer about supporting Jews;
someone said he escaped, disappeared into a dike.

Someone is whispering with a radish voice—
small and tortured, candles blown out in hearts,
castle walls ricocheting noises at night.

12.

Someone wants to rehearse a play, *As You Like It.*
How perfect to confront fear with laughter!
When the enemy approaches, they will find Shakespeare.
We work on the production and design sets
and drape them with nosegays from the garden.
We take broccoli as trumpets to announce each scene.

13.

Lately, weather has been very hot.
Perhaps, we have imagined the searchlight.
We are expecting thunderstorms
as humidity shifts its feet nervously.
We wilt in such glare.

We will have a procession through the garden
solemn as a gathering of woodchucks.
We shall have a party at 5 o'clock
when the evening cools off a little.

We will have a time of cake and coffee.
We have been hoarding these treats a long time.
It is hard to be patient when you are a child—
but hiding, pretending
we do not exist, keeping silence as a cloak,
heavy with fear, is good practice.

We will decorate the tables with heliotropes
and pennants we made from torn scraps
fastened to lamps
we cannot light for fear of exposure.

We made a play called *The Weeds Don't Die.*
We will play the parts of weeds.
Nothing can kill weeds, we say.
Not even the enemy.

We will sing until the rains arrive.
How delightful if the rain should join our singing.
Mrs. Neurse will run outside to get her baby;
both of them will return drenched as puppies.
Wulf will have to rescue our booths
erected in front of the gate. All the throwing booths
will be soggy and droopy as lost laughter.

Along will come the saturated horse wagon
with Olga and Kurt Warschauer
pretending to be farmers.
Eventually, everything will dry out.
Eventually, we will have ice cream.
No one will dream of troubles this night.

14.
September 1, 1941-April 1, 1943

Our mood dried out when the army passed near.
Our Jewish teacher, Elisabeth Schmitt,
is placed in charge of the remaining seventeen

Jewish children. No one knows
what happened to the rest. Does it matter
what date today is? Today can be any date. The rain
will fall just as hard, and death could not care.

Five children went into hiding. They searched
for the smallest place they could find.
They had experience playing *Hide and Seek.*
We heard Hans say the dogs found them
and tore them to pieces, but Hans
has a habit of saying it is raining
while standing in sunlight. We heard they survived,
but, during war, such great news
is also misleading. Often, misleading information
is how wars are started anyway.

Twelve of us children are transported to Vught
after Overijessel was declared cleansed
and fit for living. I could read the signpost
a man hung from. I turned away
from the bloated corpse
drawing flies. I changed directions,
a flower searching for light.

Now, we are told to walk the rest of the way.
I know by the sun we are headed west.
They make us walk faster. We are almost running.
I hear a gunshot. One of the children
did not run fast enough.

One of the soldiers informs their leader
a place called Auschwitz is close.

15.

We have not eaten in so long
we eat our nightmares.
We become thin shadows at noon.
We count the xylophone of our ribs.
Some of us starved to death in their sleep.
Some of us never come back from work detail.
We cannot remember what day is which.
Someone has eaten a spider.

One of the soldiers informs the Commandant
they must move—
the enemy is near.

The leader does not like this information.
He shoots the messenger.

He points his gun towards the rest of us,
the few still panting. He counts the bullets
in his cylinder. He spins it, points, and clicks.

16.

Who among us can say
this will never happen again?
The next time you see a stranger,
remember you are a stranger, too.

When you say some bad words
about a person you do not know,
remember they could be mumbling about you.

When you hear whispers,
listen how they say who does not belong here.
Remember they could say that about you.

17.

At Auschwitz, the liberating soldiers who arrived
could not decide which bothered them more:

the mass graves;
the emaciated bodies;
the piles of empty children's shoes.

There are people in this world
who deny these things ever happened.
There are people who will spread hate.

The best way to stop hate
is to not listen.

18.

All wars are the same war.

The Revolution Came Early This Winter

"I can't tell if the day is ending, or the world,
or if the secret of secrets is within me again."
—Akhimatova

*

Darkness upon darkness—some darker
than others, more purple. This is what
the world has come to—this lack of seeing, this lack of
shape and dimension, until we wonder,
were we ever here?

Who can admit seeing such a horror?

I can. I have nothing to lose. I have lost everything:
my home: my land; my love;
my love of life.

We are still being erased: memory; belief
in possibilities; kisses smaller than postage stamps.
They stamp across the heart with hooves, bee stings,
black whips, crosses burning and crying.

You want me to admit to what I saw never happened.
You want me to say that horses can pass for nighttime
when you just made me confess there is no daytime.
I can't. You have taught me to say little as possible.

*

Silence whispers my name in my ear. My name
is suspicious. If I stay low to the ground,
become snow, maybe no one will notice me.
If I wear a shawl of darkness, maybe I can blend in.

There are people taking names, turning them in.
Everyone is afraid. No one knows who to trust.
When they took you away, they destroyed your name
until I wondered if you were ever here, or if I imagined you.

When your name melted in my heart, an icicle.
From faraway your memory found me, even in hiding.
When you came, the room brightened for a second.
Not even the soldiers could drag your memory away again.

*

Who can say what is normal?

Today, a group of soldiers were marching in step,
and they had no idea where they were going
or even if they were going in the right direction.

They moved in darkness, fearing darkness,
not realizing they were the darkness.
Darkness was inside their coats, written as love letters
in case something happened. It usually does.

When one man fell behind, he was shot.
He was shot when his boot came loose.
He was shot for thinking he could fix something.
This is what the world has come to.

I found his letter to his mother.
He was too young for a girlfriend, barely twelve.
This is what war has come to. He died without knowing
love, or sunshine, or possibilities, or matches.

He died before a beard could cover his freckles.
He bled in the snow, his mouth trying to ask
for his mother, too young to do anything, really.
He died because his boots slowed him down.

When I thought of you, in the unknown,
your name was a swirl of snowflakes.
Do you remember how I unbuttoned your darkness,
kissed your fear, mailed your fear away?

The last thing you told me when they took you away
was *run,* run with snow across darkness, run
as if bees were stinging, run until you hear your hooves
as names falling off lists with everyone on them safe.

I ran, invisible, past soldiers looking for me.
I ran so fast they could not see my name was fleeing.
I took you with me. I carried you inside my heart,
my heart a soldier singing his own death before a battle.

Now both of us are escaping, my dear.
I am going where no one, except you, can find me.
When I get there, you will be there.
We will huddle together like struck matches.

There will be no more whips,
no more madness, no more mass graves,
no one searching for us anymore.
There I will be—waiting for you.

Variations of Stories I Heard in Vietnam
from the Wounded

They would be firing non-stop, for days,
the enemy would come endless as rain or breath,
there'd be this moment, not certain when,
the body and mind separated.

                                 The body would be
clenching a trigger, fingers numb, or throbbing,
or frozen, or attached, firing, eyes no longer seeing,
but seeing too clearly what was happening, accelerated
or slowed-down, heart firing endless bullets,

and alongside, a temporal spirit, perhaps the soul,
outside and transparent, disgusted, refusing to act, or
rescue, or advise, or return to the body again,

                       and now, the body was being operated on.
Sometimes, the spirit was nearby watching detached
at the incisions, sometimes, the spirit
had already walked away.

                              But when the body awoke,
it would search for the other missing half, the
human part that knew caring. The two
could not merge any more than light can join shadow,
or night with day, always longing for what could have,
what will never will be again, and needing
a different kind of healing.

Blue Battlefield

For some reason, the battlefield was blue.
The noise of bullets bent in air.
Missiles were searching for a place to shatter
and splint, the tailing waves of sound
adding final thumps to impact.

I patched the wounds under these streaks.
For some reason, I believed if I ignored the bullets,
they would overlook me. As I pressed on the blood,
I let the wounded hurtle scream after scream into the sky.
If yelling helped them, I'd let them.
There was no reason for war;
why should I think there was any rationality left?

You'd be amazed what I would do
if we ran out of bandages.

For some reason, blood reminded me of geraniums.

We would bring back anyone wounded.
Death does not discriminate, so why should we?

Sometimes the grass was blue while I carried men back.
The grass was high and thick with pain,
slowing my progress through places ignored by reason.

I would return, find some more, bring them back.
I was a metronome.

Not everyone survived, either on the field or in surgery.
However, there would always be some who survived.
If I helped some to live, they were one less body for Death.
And I returned, irrationally, into the blue deadly light.

Open Wounds

Bullets never touched me.
Under explosions, flashbacks,
the sky weltering, skinned alive,
I lifted the dead-weight of the wounded half-bodies
across the *pop-pop-pop,* elusive land.

Some soldiers counted days to going home;
I counted bodies saved; bodies mutilated.
Life was rationed. I moved under fire: elusive smoke.
Days passed as my hands tried to staunch blood.

In Vietnam, the sky was the color of a green tent,
it would be weeks of rain, fine as rice.
When I found extra arms or legs or feet or hands,
doctors asked: *Do you expect us to reattach them?*

Time never mattered. War grounded salt into wounds.
Days began with reddish-dark blood sunsets,
and ended with bandaged moonlights.

Women in black silk clothes
searched among the dead and dying, trying to identify
who belonged to them, and when there was a match,
wails cut air with helicopter blades.

                          *

My son was learning about the Vietnam War.
His teacher did not understand war.
He was never there. He'd never seen a body
against the background flash of napalm,
an x-ray. He'd never seen a man die,
intestine snaking out. I'd been back twenty years
and never said I was there. No one knew. I never said.
Words were disconnected from experience.
I was livid with the teacher.
I had to give him a piece of my mind. I showed him
the scars on my feet and arms from the skin grafts.
He became sick. I told him about children with stumps.
I laid into him. His face surrendered. I had gone too far.

This is why I never told anyone. I went silent
for another twenty years, a submarine going deep.

How far is too far? The war went too far
for some, not far enough for others. They never saw
a child in flames from napalm, never saw how

months-long monsoon still could not wash

blood from the field. I still have more questions,
no answers.

*

Not long after I returned, wounded and limping,
I met a Vietnamese woman, and we started a conversation.
She knew from my accent where I had been.
She asked about her family *back there*; I never met them.

I had two choices: I could lie and say I knew them,
or I could disappoint her. Her vocabulary had questions
songbirding. I wanted her to nest in my hands.

She wanted some news, but all I knew was damage control.
The more I wanted to be with her, the more I knew
they were all the wrong reasons;
I was used to handling wounds. I was still a lit fuse.

I never answered her. I never knew her name.
I listened to the music of her questions, and for once,
she seemed to know someone was just listening.
l listened to her soft rain. Her face opened up
like an umbrella, and the sun, I swear, exploded.

All day, she rained questions.

*

A survivor and I accidentally met thirty years later.
He remembered me. He had a new prosthesis.
He showed me the new one was better
than the one we'd given him,
which we jury-rigged from spare parts.
He had questions. The wounded always want answers.

I remembered when he cursed me
after he noticed that his arm was gone.
He wanted to thank me now.
He told me about going home. His girl
had run off with another man. Then he met his wife;
he actually felt he had a better deal.
Things worked out that way. I listened
but wanted to get going. I was uncomfortable.
He wanted to trade war stories; I wanted out of there.
I did not want to talk about it.

I had a simple mission: rescue as many as I could.

*

When I returned, going out daily was a chore.
I was suspicious of quiet.
When my son played with toy soldiers,
I wanted to tell him about needing a medic,
then thought better of it. Play and imagination
should be not painted with reality.

It took me over forty years to face what I saw.
Not only painful to handle the dying
(and it was), but hard to admit
I had anything to do with survival.

I carried the wounded, held them open
during operations, fitted them with prosthetics,
zipped the body bags.

Nothing much, I thought, *considering.*

Forty Years Later

I am still   in Vietnam
            still as a crane in field marsh
when the uneven sunset reflected on the lake

I am giving an emergency tracheotomy
                        on the twisted ruins of a body

the ripped open chest cavity of earth is a foxhole

            I am back there again   and again
a revolving tour of duty
in the ward of bandages and pain
                        with no viable exit strategy

ducks glide   Baby Huey helicopters
in reverence—   *in coming*

            bodies stacked
                        compressing wounds
                                    clouds of intestines unraveling

            if I was a crane
I would have taken off
                        lifted my body out of the experience
transparent as the skin exploding

name tags are absent   or assigned wrongly
            all bodies are the same body
                        bone fragment memory
black plastic bags purses
            not sure which arm belongs where

I am still crawling though bodies interminably
                        numb as a grenade

            I have to remind myself
I am no longer there   but here

                        miles and years away from carnage

the bed I crawl into   is not a foxhole

The Miles Before Sleep

I did something hard: I stared at my mother
on a ventilator, lungs working overtime.
The end was in her sight, the shortening miles
before she could pull over and rest.

Her eyes were begging, *Make it end.*
I looked into her eyes, trying to pull her back,
until I saw she wanted to drown
in silence. She had provided birth, and now
she craved death as if death was a candy bar.

She was evaporating into her skin, a prayer,
fingers on a rosary, her road map
indicating miles to go before arriving.

I didn't look away from observing death.
There is no shame in dying, no dishonor
in remorse, no journey without someone looking back.
She gazed straight into the nowhere, terrorized
at what was next. Religion had warned her
about heaven and hell, simple sins
leading to confession booths, scabbing the knees.

I began talking to her in both mundane
and important words, a chattering magpie.
And my voice might reassure her, telling her
she could leave, that I would be fine.

I have seen the eyes of surrender in Vietnam.
Death is not explosive as a minefield,
nor zipped silent in a body bag,
nor always gory, but always the eyes
are unable to say what they wanted to say.
When they are doped up on morphine, they can't speak,
can't name their fear: sad eyes, seen-it-all eyes
tired-of-battlefields or common-problems eyes,
same eyes needing comfort.

NEW POEMS

Blending In, Phasing Out, a Wrinkle of Silence

During the pitchforked darkness, the cows seem beyond restless,
rustling their tails and bellowing.
It takes a disturbance to upset innocence. I enter the barn
without a lit lantern, trying to catch the intruder with surprise.
I sense the spark-arm-prick danger; wildness leaping and arcing.

I rub the cows' flanks, partly to sooth them, partly
to feel my way without light.
I taste anxiety: the cows; the predator; mine.

The unseen slides quietly like the barn door: shape-shifting fear.
I have to out-wait whatever lurches in the unseen.
I use the hunter's trick of blending in:
going so silent, easing the heartrate, a kind of meditation,
until I almost disappear.

I become less noise than a cow's tail hushing swish, swish.

The unseen offers a truce, not wanting to be captured or killed.
It leaves, a wrinkle of silence, and the cows settle down.

I return to the house, still quaking, not knowing what I avoided,
what lurked in the unknown, how close danger arrived,
unseen, barely detectable.

How to Be Welcomed into the Universe
and How to Invite Others to Join

The only way forward in the summer's high-pitch frog trills
starts with standing still. Stay within throb-pulse volume
until it affects our blood flow, all the way
to violet-purple before night. Wait
for desire to happen. Add to the frog excitement
the leaf-stir, the river-flow.
Wait for the stars to appear from clouds
like sleepy children yawning. During this late hour,
every sound softens any terrible story,
the universe murmurs with frog-echoes,
chanting and naming their incredible desires.
One step into this magic will never be enough.
It will be alright if we stay longer, return more often.

Ode to a Loom

I am not supposed to know the loom, nor the shuttle
sliding between two pieces of fabric
like light between Venetian blind slats.
I am not supposed to hear praise whisper
as I slide the shuttle to make what I see in my mind,
what my fingers see when pulling the fabric.
I am not supposed to feel my name mentioned
on the fabric that I spun from wool, spun so fine
like long silken hair, thinner than spider's web.
I am not supposed to sit here, my feet on the pedal
to pull, tighten, snap the fabric together. I am not
what you expect. My hands slip like fabric, smooth
as light on a spider's web, spun singing
from an orb spider. I am not supposed to hear that noise.
It's the same as light rising through cloud-fabric,
leaf fiber, songs of merging of pieces into a whole,
all designed by imagination, guided by my hands.
No, I am not supposed to be performing this composition.
Someone declares this woman's work. I enter the secret world
of making and stitching, shuttling words between fabric.
My hands know how to make from nothing, to create.
The wooden frame moves with snap and relapse, tug,
tighten, release. My hands speak "treadle," "warp," "weft."
I am not supposed to shuttle these words, this thread I spun
on a spindle. All language flows like silk thread
between the slat of my fingers. The loom does not judge me.
It declares: *snap fabric together. Make what you see.*
I see the fabric of love, of merging, light rising over horizons,
flights of sparrows, songs of leaves whisking in wind.
I do this work slowly. I shuttle the opposite way,
carry the work through to the start, to why
I am not supposed to know the loom. The shuttle goes back
and forth, like day to night to day to finish to start.
I am not supposed to know this, not supposed to hear
the fabric singing: *make me into something useful.*
Sure. I will make you something useful, with purpose,
with intention, with attention to detail—see your emergence
like a newborn, like first birdsong, like world's creation.
I am not supposed to know this. I am not supposed to do this work.
My hands ask why not. My imagination says I can, I will.

Kaddish

My grandmother asks me to touch Grandfather's corpse,
so that I might know death's mercy, death's eternal promise.
A body feels cold and hard when it empties into a hollowness.

This ridged journey is something I thought I understood,
but this is not the same as slaughtering a cow,
draining its blood, cleaving it into cuts.

This place is where Grandfather cleared the land and accepted death.
In a few hours Grandmother joins him,
dying while holding my hand.

I hand-craft their coffins, dig their graves when the county said
they belonged in a pauper's grave. I engrave her coffin
with primroses and his with forget-me-nots.

I bury them in the dark of night,
never say where I did. I bury them
before the bank could foreclose the land.

There are moments that belong to death
and don't belong to taxes; moments to ignore rules;
moments belonging to prayer and carving secrecy.

I brush off the wood shavings and fresh dirt from my hands.
I don't know Kaddish,
but I think this is how it must go.

The Search

My grandfather's Guernsey escaped the barn,
and he never figured out how. She wandered out
into a full-blown snow gale, her trail
vanishing under more bright
and trembling whiteness.
The cow must have left hours earlier,
as untraceable as a rumor out of control.

My grandfather went out into the blizzard,
his lantern light bounding and bouncing
on the knee-high snow, towards the far woods
drenched in accumulating, suffocating snow.

That's all that could be asked,
all that could be expected: hunting in snowdrifts,
calling into the snowstorm, toes going numb,
risking frostbite or hyperthermia.

He never found the cow that night, or the next,
or the futile weeks thereafter, until he gave up
searching, letting nature take its cruel turn.

In summer, he found the cow's carcass by accident.
There wasn't much left to identify.
It wasn't hard to puzzle out. Bones had a tale to tell:
the world judged harshly such carelessness.

Grandfather lived close to that edge,
witnessing things that went wrong.
Moments can end bad, quickly. All time needed
is just one mistake between birth and early death.

Hope was his lantern trying to find the lost.
Every action and reaction prepared him
for what to do next time and how to absorb failure.

Boats Sailing in Uncharted Territory

I receive a phone call: *your father is dying.*
It's like easing a boat into choppy water.

I'm not going to make it in time
when I'm across the country in Georgia.
If I want to say goodbye or say thanks
for the memories, it's half too-late.
He arrives at the hospital half-dead,
dies the rest of the way.

They say he saw his death coming for months,
and no one wanted to concern me. Memory thanks
anyone who cares. It's a nasty hot Georgia
November, and deer move tentative
through heart monitors, halving time.

They just want me to know, I do not have to worry,
he eased into death like they were bed slippers.
The news anchors deep. Memory halves.

In half-light, the phone makes no sense.
I forget to ask why they withheld the news.
I drop whatever I am doing. *Too late*
is always the worse news for memory to hear.

It's almost funny the terms we use
to avoid saying directly someone is dead:
he passed away; it was his time; it's better this way.

They say they will hold up the funeral until I arrive.

I am four hours from the nearest airport. I drive
through the night and Georgia heat
like a directional arrow.
They say I'll laugh about this someday.
I do not see the humor in any of this day.

Boats going out does not mean boats returning;
some boats vanish

where ocean and horizon blends.

The Universal Sign for Silence
Is a Hush Finger to the Lips

A soothing drizzle—sounds of stillness,
what are you trying to tell me?

My deaf father was not born deaf.
He lost his hearing in a war.
He refuses to learn sign language.

Rain, why does silence have so many languages?

A rain not heard is still rain. In sign,
I loosely filter fingers downward for *rain.*
Rain is a verb.

Father wanted words filtered
into long-faced vowels, forced
and explosive consonants.
He wants me to shape words with my mouth.
Words as verbs.

The sign for *stubborn* is cross your arms and pout.
Children know this one. Father refuses to learn it.
Father holds the dictionary of silence.

He knows stillness has a beating heart,
and just because he can't hear sound doesn't mean
it isn't everywhere. Silence hurts.

I know the sign for *pain.*
I hit a fist into an open palm and make a face.

The sign for *love* is a heart traveling to another.

The Shirt

I wait for rain to pass before taking laundry out.
The rusty creak pulleys
move a line of clothes further when wet,
nearer when dry. My father is waiting.
The laundry will smell of lilacs
and front doors opening.

I shake loose the laundry before folding,
stacking them in a wicker basket.
I snap sheets into distant thunder.

I lay out my father's shirt,
fold its arms over the front,
hugging the shape of emptiness. I fold again,
neck to belly buttonhole.
I even button the shirt before folding.
I pack neatly.
My father is waiting.

I lay out my father's shirt and iron.
The breast pocket will hold
his off-white monogram handkerchief.
I fold the edges of the handkerchief
into the silence.

I take his shirt as an offering to the undertaker.
Father would prefer this pale blue dress shirt.

All Night I Harvest Your Name

All night, the wind teaches the branches
how to write your name,
and a thousand eyes witness their writing
with soft river-sounds.

All night, sand grains murmur your name,
shifting each vowel,
trying out each sound, their smoothness
like the plush-velvet skies
as the night begins its aria.

Yes, all night, there is the dissembling
of ideas because I'm searching for you.

Although the world is vast and faceless,
and occasionally meteors streak across
blazing your name,
I can't find you.

All night, all night, crickets brim
excitedly, repeating your name—

your name of serious translations, a name
purpling into nightfall, a wing-full of a name
into an uncommon wind.

I ask the great horned owl,
and he admits he doesn't know who you are.

When the wind rushes your name
against my window, I open the blinds,
and I can see fire and water mixing together.

If I ignore your name,
your name might turn into foam, pull back
into the ocean of many names,
because whatever is freely given
can be taken back. All night, I worry about this.
All night, I write your name feverishly in my heart.

I write your name in the shadows between rose petals.
I write your name into the green world
almost broken by possible loss.

~

Acknowledgments

These poems were published in the following journals or anthologies, to whose editors grateful acknowledgment is given.

About Place: "Ile Aux Fleurs"
Adelaide Literary Journal: "Love Is Never Far from Us"
Ancient Paths: "The Insistent Knocking"
Autumn Sky Poetry Daily: "April 17," "The Miles Before Sleep," "The Sound Water Makes," "Variations of Stories I heard in Vietnam from the Wounded"
Bagel Bards #6 (anthology): "Psalm: There is a passing, calling me from somewhere"
Be About It: "Gardening in Georgia Clay"
Big City Lit: "Before Words," "Too Soon the Clouds of Disenchanted Rains Will Be Upon Us"
Big River Review: "Tor House," "The Transitory World"
Blue Fifth Review: "The Midday Nap"
Bigger Stones: "The Letter"
Black Poppy Review: "Loss"
Blue Fifth Review: "Searching for What Is Not There"
Broadkill River Review: "Coming Home Celebration"
Centrifugal Eye: "For My First Wife Who Died on a Late August Day Much Like Today," "Sudden Chill"
Cherry Blossom Review: "Repairs and More Repairs"
Comstock Review: "The Universal Sign for Silence Is a Hush Finger to the Lips"
Dead Snakes: "Coming from a Dark County"
Flutter Poetry Journal: "Farm Road," "In the Presence of Absence," "Psalm: All day, inside me, your voice was saying"
Furnace: "Psalm: How wonderful the spirit," "Psalm: How to be intimate with the world"
Hotmetalpress.net: "The Harmony of the Found," "Mending More Than Socks"
Identity Crisis: "Before Letters"
Istanbul Literary Review: "How to Be Silent," "Listen"
JWMM: "Song of the Bottomless Lament"
Kentucky Review: "Dylan Thomas at the Writing Shed"
Lantern Lit: "Crows Are Not Afraid to Talk About Death"
Leaf Garden Press: "Maple and Cedar; Lake George"
Muddy River Poetry Review: "Cow Barn"
Nixes Mate Review: "The Search"
Numinous: "Untitled (Being in the Presence is more than the here and now)," "When Stillness Is Heard"
Poetrybay: "This Is What We Cannot See"
Poetry in the Cathedral (anthology): "What Happens When in Stillness"
Poppy Road Review: "The Lawrence Tree," "Pelvis IV"

Punkin House (slumber theme): "The River of Forgetfulness," "What Will Happen If We Pull Down the Empty Sky"

Red Poppy Review: "Seeing Like Never Before," "What It Is like to Go into Silent Meditation"

Red Wolf Journal: "How Leaves Form," "Lamentation for a Natural World," "Swan"

Sin Fronteras: "Wakening"

The Song Is...: "Braids"

Soul-Lit: "Untitled (Psalm: as close as any two molecules)"

These Fragile Lilacs: "Silence Has Its Own Language"

Tipton Poetry Journal: "Knowing the Answer"

Verse-Virtual: "Blue Battlefield"

Wilderness House Literary Review: "Rapture," "This Is What Happens When Your Name Is Called and You Missed Your Turn," "The Universe Has a Sermon about Remembrance"

Written River: "Early Autumn at Itako," "This Pond Has Clear Imaginings"

"Daffodils" won the Dylan Thomas International Poetry Award, 2014.

"Glass Walls Do Not a Barrier Make" was the winner of the 2013 National Broadsided Contest (theme: Typhoon Haiyan 2013). This contest was to match Joel Haber's artwork.

"How to Be Silent" was reprinted in the anthology *Gathered: Contemporary Quaker Poets* (Sundress Press, 2013).

"Improvisations in Darkness" was published as a chaplet, *Improvisations in Darkness* (Origami Poetry Project, 2014).

"In the Beginning We Tumble into Light" appeared in the anthology, *Meditations on Divine Names* (Moonrise Press, 2012).

"The Little Gardeners" appeared in the anthology, *Collateral Damage* (Glass Lyre Press, 2018).

"Mending the Net" was reprinted in the anthology *The Heart of all That Is: Reflections on Home* (Holy Cow! Press, 2013).

"On a Starry Night," appeared in the anthology, *Tranquility* (Kind of Hurricane Press, 2016).

"Open Wounds" won the 2018 Stephen A. DiBiase Poetry Prize.

"The Revolution Came Early This Winter" appeared in the anthology, *Carrying the Branch: World Peace Anthology* (Glass Lyre Press, 2018).

"Some Days" appeared in the anthology, *A Roof of Red Tiles & other stories & poems* (Cinnamon Press, 2014).

"The Sounds of Color" and "Touch Is Something We All Need" appeared in the anthology, *In Terra Pax* (Cinnamon Press, 2011).

"Tor House" was nominated Poem of the Month: August 2013 and also for a 2013 Pushcart Prize by *Big River Poetry Review*.

"What the Soundlessness Is Telling Us" appeared in the chaplet, *When We Are in the Moment* (Origami Poetry Project, 2019).

About FutureCycle Press

FutureCycle Press is dedicated to publishing lasting English-language poetry in both print-on-demand and Kindle formats. Founded in 2007 by long-time independent editor/publishers and partners Diane Kistner and Robert S. King, the press was incorporated as a nonprofit in 2012. A number of our editors are distinguished poets and writers in their own right, and we have been actively involved in the small press movement going back to the early seventies.

Each year, we have awarded the FutureCycle Poetry Book Prize and honorarium for the best original full-length volume of poetry by a single author that we published that year; if no original collections are published, no prize is offered. Introduced in 2013, proceeds from our Good Works projects are donated to charity. Our Selected Poems series highlights contemporary poets with a substantial body of work to their credit; with this series we strive to resurrect work that has had limited distribution and is now out of print.

We are dedicated to giving all of the authors we publish the care their work deserves, offering a catalog of the most diverse and distinguished work possible, and paying forward any earnings to fund more great books. All of our books are kept "alive" and available unless and until an author requests a title be taken out of print.

We've learned a few things about independent publishing over the years. We've also evolved a unique and resilient publishing model that allows us to focus mainly on vetting and preserving for posterity poetry collections of exceptional quality without becoming overwhelmed with bookkeeping and mailing, fundraising activities, or taxing editorial and production "bubbles." To find out more, come see us at futurecycle.org.

www.ingramcontent.com/pod-product-compliance
Lightning Source LLC
Chambersburg PA
CBHW072142090426
42739CB00013B/3255